BIG DATA AND ANALYTICS

SAMIYA KHAN

INDIA • SINGAPORE • MALAYSIA

Notion Press Media Pvt Ltd

No. 50, Chettiyar Agaram Main Road,
Vanagaram, Chennai, Tamil Nadu – 600 095

First Published by Notion Press 2022

ISBN 979-8-88530-487-0

TABLE OF CONTENTS

PREFACE

"Big data is at the foundation of all of the megatrends that are happening today, from social to mobile to the cloud to gaming."

– Chris Lynch

Data deluge has been one of the biggest concerns for the scientific community in recent times. As a result of mass digitization across domains and borders, the data pool became huge. Thus, the traditional systems for storage and processing were overwhelmed by this humongous data reservoir.

Organizations were forced to decide whether to discard this data or archive it. A decision in favor of maintaining a data reserve can be attributed to the fact that this data is capable of steering many organization-level decisions and revolutionizing how problem-solving and decision-making are performed.

In a popular article by Chris Anderson, Editor, Wired Magazine, it was explained how the scientific method, in itself, has become obsolete in the big data era. The foundation of a scientific method for solving problems lies in proposing a hypothetical solution to a problem and collecting data to test the proposed solution. However, in the present time and age, we have lots of data, and instead of looking for solutions to problems, we are looking for problems that can be solved using the data heap available to us.

Big data has changed the equation most remarkably. Since data is the heart and soul of this technology, its applicability is extensive. Therefore, Big data is being used in varied streams, from Geo-Statistics to Bioinformatics. Personalized medicine and smart cities have been the most accepted real-life endeavors of big data technologies.

As we traverse the journey of big data from the inception of this concept to its present-day position in the market, Hadoop has been a constant feature on the big data technologies list. Furthermore, Hadoop has also evolved with the changing demands and market understanding with solutions such as Spark to expand its capabilities and become a complete big data framework for application development.

This book is a beginner's guide to big data and Hadoop. It has been organized in such a manner that it describes the big data problem and need for Hadoop. Henceforth, all the components of the Hadoop ecosystem are individually covered. Chapter 1 to Chapter 9 provides theory lessons, while Chapter 10 to Chapter 20 are lab tutorials that can be aligned with theory chapters to better understand the subject. The theory and practical coverage of the book shall help the reader connect the dots between the different processes of the big data lifecycle, facilitating the development of comprehensive solutions for complex big data problems. First, Chapter 1 introduces the big data problem and gives an eagle's eye view of Hadoop, a distributed programming framework. Besides this, it also provides a comparison between Hadoop and RDBMS.

Chapter 2 dwells deeper into the Hadoop Ecosystem and HDFS Architecture. There are two Hadoop versions available, Hadoop 1.x and Hadoop 2.x. This chapter points out the differences between these two versions and describes the key components of the Hadoop Ecosystem. Storage and processing are the two main functions of Hadoop. In order to understand how Hadoop performs these functions, Cluster Architecture and YARN are explained in detail. In addition to this, basic Hadoop functions like data placement, reading, and writing are explained in detail with the help of sequence diagrams. Finally, it also mentions the cluster modes in which Hadoop operates and the configuration files that can be changed to modify the operational characteristics of the system.

MapReduce programming paradigm is implemented using Hadoop. First, the basics of this programming paradigm and its comparison with the conventional form of programming are described in Chapter 3. Then, the workflows for application execution and job submission are diagrammatically explained. Finally, a working example of MapReduce code is provided to better understand the concept. This chapter aims to help the reader understand how the MapReduce programming paradigm can be implemented in Hadoop using Java programming language.

Chapter 4 builds on the foundations of MapReduce programming laid in the previous chapter. Advanced programming concepts like Input Splits, Partitioner, Combiner, Counters, and Input Formats are discussed in this chapter. In addition, Map and Reduce Side Joins are also explained, along with a discussion on which type of Join operation must be implemented in what kind of a programming scenario. Lastly, this chapter demonstrates the need and use of MRUnit Testing Framework, a debugging tool commonly used for MapReduce code.

Companies like Yahoo and Facebook use Hadoop at the backend to perform analysis of their data. However, their data analysts are not well versed with NoSQL and usually have little to no expert knowledge of advanced programming languages. As a result, abstraction tools like Pig and Hive have been developed to reduce the programming effort required for performing common data analytical tasks. Chapter 5 is dedicated to Pig, providing a complete theoretical background of the tool to the reader. Topics like key characteristics, performance issues, limitations, and applications are covered. Besides this, the basics of Pig scripting are also elucidated.

Although Pig and Hive are two tools solving the same purpose, they are two dissimilar solutions developed by different companies. The differences between Pig and Hive are elaborated upon in Chapter 6. Moreover, Hive is also compared with traditional RDBMS to provide a holistic view to the reader. Finally, Hive architecture, components, limitations, and scripting are explained to provide the reader with enough knowledge about the tool to get started with the practical aspects of the same.

Chapter 7 is a detailed description of NoSQL Databases and their classification. HBase is the NoSQL solution available as part of the Hadoop ecosystem. However, users can integrate other NoSQL solutions with Hadoop to achieve better performance. Because of this reason, NoSQL, as a complete topic, is discussed. The chapter focuses on HBase, covering its basic concepts, uses components, and storage architecture. Zookeeper is additionally covered as part of this chapter because of its inseparable association with HBase processes. Lastly, basic working knowledge of HBase is provided to help the reader get started with its practical facets.

Oozie is the top-most level component of the Hadoop ecosystem that allows developers to specify workflows or set of Hadoop tasks that need to be performed sequentially to perform a specific task. If a task requires repeated execution, then specifying the workflow and instructing Oozie to time the execution of the workflow as per development requirements can prove to be extremely performance-effective. Chapter 8 explains Oozie and its functional component, highlighting how jobs can be scheduled using this component of Hadoop.

Hadoop is an effective framework for distributed data processing. However, it lacks the statistical and analytical capabilities required to perform complex big data issues. On the other hand, R is an open-source programming language designed for data analysis, providing a plethora of packages to solve key analytical problems. Thus, integrating R with Hadoop is an effective approach to developing big data solutions. Chapter 9 describes the feasibility of R and Hadoop integration, explaining useful methods for convenient assimilation.

The rest of the chapters (Chapter 10-20) are lab tutorials, with Chapter 10 and Chapter 11 providing installation and setup instructions for standalone and multi-node cluster ensembles, respectively. Chapter 12 introduces HDFS commands, which is a crucial tutorial because it provides a basic working knowledge of the system to the reader. Finally, basic and advanced MapReduce programming and implementation are elucidated in Chapters 13 and 14.

Lab tutorials corresponding to Pig, Hive, HBase, and Oozie are provided in Chapter 15, Chapter 16, Chapter 17, and Chapter 18, respectively. In order to process data, it needs to be imported into HDFS. Hadoop can be integrated with two tools, namely Sqoop and Flume, to import structured and unstructured data, respectively. Chapter 19 describes how these two tools can be used for importing data. The last chapter suggests project ideas and their proposed implementation for readers to realize and apply on their own. At the end of every chapter, multiple-choice, short answer, and long answer questions for self-evaluation.

Realizing the potential of big data and Hadoop in the development and evolution of user-centric and problem-specific solutions, these technologies feature highly on the list of industry-relevant skills. Therefore, this book can be extremely helpful for students, researchers, and faculty, and industry professionals to get started with their big data journey.

Samiya Khan

ACKNOWLEDGMENTS

The making of a book is a long journey that spans several years of hard work, patience, and persistence. I owe my focus and determination to my people's guidance, encouragement, and sacrifices. So, I would like to take this opportunity to express my heartfelt gratitude to my family, friends, and colleagues for their endless support throughout this journey.

This book would not have been possible without my mentor and PhD supervisor, *Dr Mansaf Alam*. I would also like to thank *Dr Syed Shafat Ali*, *Dr Kashish Ara Shakil*, *Dr Arif Anwar*, and *Dr Zafaryab Rasool* for reviewing the manuscript and providing their valuable feedback. My alma mater, *Jamia Millia Islamia*, is where I started my research journey and will always be where I belong. I am forever thankful to this institution of knowledge for making me the academic and person I am today.

I would particularly like to acknowledge the support and encouragement from my parents, without whom I would have never embarked on this academic journey in the first place. Furthermore, I would like to extend my gratitude to my brother, *Savvy Hasan Khan*, for saving my day on several occasions and my daughter, *Noor*, for being such a good baby and letting me finish all I started. Finally, I would like to make a special mention of *Adv Abdul Tahir Khan* for putting up with my idiosyncrasies and being a source of inspiration.

Lastly, I wish to acknowledge and appreciate the Notion Press team for their continuous support throughout the entire process of publication. Finally, my gratitude is extended to the readers, who gave me their trust, and I hope this work guides and inspires them.

I dedicate this book to my family.

Samiya Khan

Chapter 1

INTRODUCTION TO BIG DATA AND HADOOP

OBJECTIVES

- Big data definition
- Limitations of existing architectures
- Solving existing issues with Hadoop
- Introduction to Hadoop
- Difference between RDBMS and Hadoop

1.1 BIG DATA CONCEPT

Digitization and the emergence of social media portals have increased the amount of data available on the Internet and devices manifold. Moreover, this data is increasing daily at an alarming rate. As a result, traditional systems cannot manage and process this data. The challenges and issues posed by such scenarios are cumulatively termed as the 'big data problem.'

Big data is an elusive concept used to describe the challenge of handling vast amounts of data. Therefore, any data that cannot be handled, managed, and/or processed by an organization's existing infrastructure can be termed big data. On the other hand, Hadoop is a framework that provides a solution to the big data problem. Big data is 'big' not just in terms of volume but also in terms of complexity. Data typically of the order of terabytes and petabytes is referred to as big data, with other key characteristics such as variety and velocity also considered for classification.

1.1.1 Background

The strategic use of data to track and monitor businesses is as ancient as it can get. The first recorded usage dates 7000 years back when the concept of accounting was used for herd management by the Mesopotamians. The evolution of this field has remained gradual since then. For example, it was only in 1663 that John Grunt became the first person in history to record and examine data for studying mortality roles in London.

Intuitively, this field caught up and garnered global attention after the digital revolution. Thus, the earliest remembrances of modern data date back to 1887, when Herman Hollerith invented the computing machine. The 20th century marked the dawn of the 'Information Age,' and Fig. 1.1 illustrates the evolution of technology within this timeline. Since then, the rapid evolution of computing and storage infrastructures has changed the landscape of data collection, processing, archival, and analysis. However, Big Data got a formalized identity in 2005 when Roger Douglas coined the term Big Data, and Yahoo came up with the first big data processing platform Hadoop.

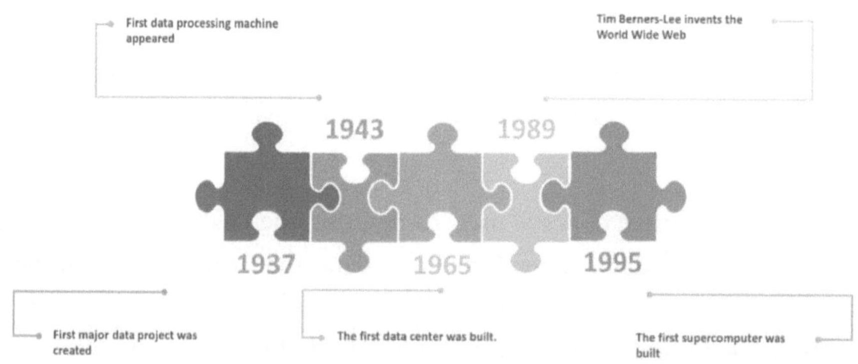

Fig. 1.1 20th Century Timeline

Data is increasing at an alarming rate. According to a study, the volumetric estimate of big data is expected to reach 180 zettabytes by 2025. To help you understand how big this is, consider this scenario as an example. If you want to download all the data available in the world through the Internet, it will take you almost 181 million years to do so.

Big data gives us the power to collect and harness the potential of this ever-increasing reserve in understanding the world and everything that lies within it. However, if big data has existed for so long, why are we talking about it so much now? As the famous metaphor goes, the total is always more significant than the sum of its parts. The applicability of big data analytics is no longer limited to science and has found innovative applications in diverse domains such as financial analytics, weather forecasting, healthcare applications, and forensic sciences (Fig. 1.2), to name a few.

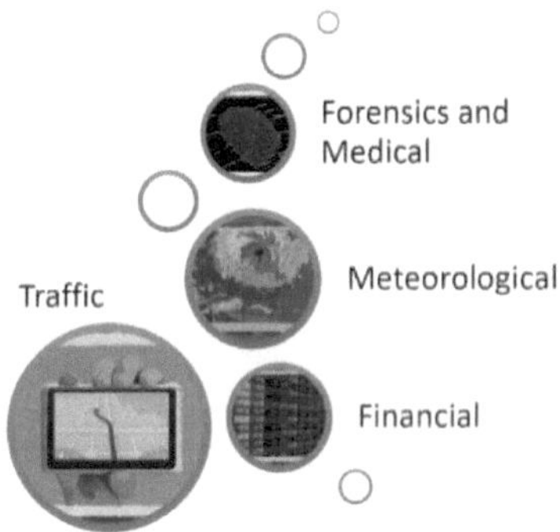

Fig. 1.2 Application Domains of Big Data

1.1.2 Scalability: A Big Data Requirement

Big data is 'big' and complex, and in order to store, process, and visualize this data, we need systems that can handle these requirements without getting overwhelmed. Thus, the scalability requirement of systems is in reference to the volume and complexity of data being processed. With the increased volume, the solution must remain valid and work with comparable, if not better, effectiveness and efficiency. Moreover, if the requirements of the application mandate real-time processing of incoming data, the solution must remain valid with variations in the amount of data being ingested.

1.1.3 Example: Stock Market

One of the best scenarios that generate big data is the stock market. The generation of data in these scenarios is of the order of terabytes per day. This data is typically used for generating insights, patterns, and predictions. However, before any such analysis can be generated, this data needs to be acquired, stored, and processed. Storage is an essential aspect because stock markets generate data all the time, and for analysis, effective data storage and management are crucial steps. Therefore, big data solutions developed need reliable storage and fast data processing.

1.1.4 Types of Data

Big data includes three types of data, which are as follows –

- Structured data
    - Data can be fitted into the standard table and column format.
    - Example: ERP and CRM data
- Unstructured data
    - Data does not have a structure or format.
    - Example:
        - Archived documents
        - Social media data

          There is no set value or a range of values that the fields can take; for example, comments on Facebook can be anything and need not be a simple yes-no or images)
- Semi-Structured Data
    - Data is partly structured and partly unstructured.
    - Example: JSON, XML and Emails

      An email has a broad structure in the form of 'Sender, Recipient, Subject, and Body', but the contents of these blocks can be unstructured.

1.2 IBM'S 3V MODEL

Three characteristics describe big data: volume, variety, and velocity, as described in Fig. 1.3. Volume, as the name suggests, describes the size of data. This data may be generated on a regular or periodic basis. The speed at which data is generated is described as data velocity. Besides this, data may include images, audio, video, text, and logs. This facet of big data is labeled as data variety.

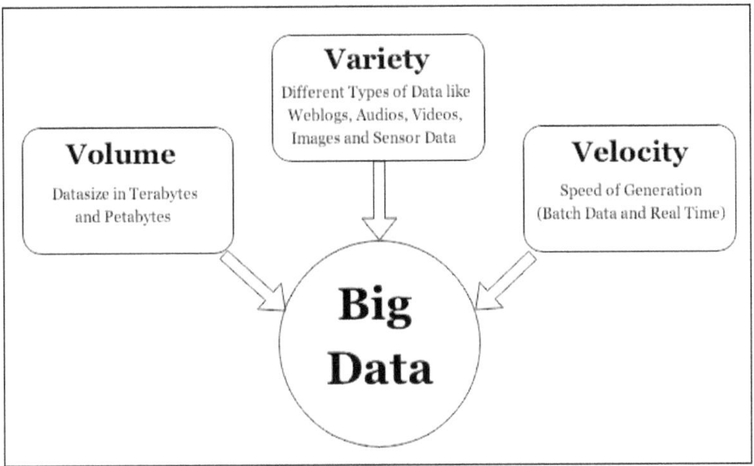

Fig. 1.3 Big Data Model

The standard 3V model has been extended to include three more V's, namely, veracity, value, and viability, and can be understood as follows –

1. Veracity

   Veracity deals with variations in data or reliability or accuracy of data being captured. The tool created must be able to handle these variations in data. Examples of veracity include missing values and format inconsistencies.

2. Value

   Companies archive all kinds of data. However, not all of this data may be of use to the system. Therefore, the tool must identify data that is of 'value.'

3. Viability

   Identifying variables that can benefit and thereby assessing the proposed solution's 'viability' is also one of the main tasks of the tool concerned.

Many advanced models have been proposed in research to describe big data and introduce new V's to the existing model.

1.3 HOW CAN BIG DATA BENEFIT BUSINESSES

A real-life example of how big data and Hadoop is of benefit can be seen in Amazon Services. If you have ever purchased on Amazon, you would know that Amazon comes up with recommendations for you, giving a list of other items that you may like to buy as soon as you make a purchase. Also, keeping the privacy issues at bay, if Amazon can get Twitter data and process it, it will know the people you follow on Twitter.

For example, if you follow an author or a celebrity and there is a new book by the author or on the celebrity, it will be recommended to you. There is a high chance you will be interested in this recommendation and consider buying the book. In reality, most such recommendations convert into purchases. Such technological interventions enhance business for Amazon in a unique way that mutually benefits Amazon as well as the customer.

Recommendations are presented even to users who just login to Amazon. Therefore, Amazon needs to get access to your other profiles and analyze your search history, buying history, profile data to get you suggestions even before seeing your profile page. Hadoop backs such batch processing. This technology opens doors for you to get the best out of big data and benefit from its potential for better business insights and research opportunities.

1.4 HADOOP AND ITS APPLICATIONS

The big data concept started with Google. At Google, scientists wanted to get all the data on the Internet to the Google platform and make it available on the Google Search Engine. They faced two challenges in their attempts to do so: storage and processing. To solve these, they came up with GFS (Google File System) and MapReduce and published them as white papers. Later on, GFS became an inspiration for the development of HDFS, and MapReduce ended up as Hadoop MapReduce. These are part of the Apache project (open source) now.

Some of the applications of Hadoop include –

- eBay
  eBay records all the search and buying/selling at the backend. This data is analyzed for recommendation engines, ad targeting, improved search quality, and abuse and click fraud detection.
- Telecommunication
  Typical applications include failure detection.
- Govt. Sector
  A popular project that is a case study for big data is the Aadhar Project initiated by the Government of India.
- Life Sciences and Medical Sciences
  Big data technologies are primarily used for research (e.g., gene sequencing).
- Banking
  Fraud detection is one of the most popular big data applications in the banking sector.
- Retail
  The retail sector is driven by sentiment analysis. The use of big data for this purpose can improve the results substantially.

1.5 LIMITATIONS OF EXISTING ARCHITECTURES

With standard technologies like Oracle, SAS, and Teradata, most companies and organizations could not scale solutions, and data processing took as much time as equivalent to a few weeks. Data is collected and appended into Storage Grid (original raw data). ETL is run on this data, which is aggregated to generate corresponding reports. Problems that arise using traditional technologies have been illustrated in Fig. 1.4 and are as follows –

1. Premature death of data occurs because we do not have the mechanism to support analysis of such large amounts of data. So, only about 10% of the data can be used. If you look at it from a statistics point of view, then the larger the data, the better the result! In other words, the smaller the dataset used for analysis gets, the more limited and constrained your results will be because they do not consider the complete scenario and dataset.
2. Typically, data is moved to a common point where computation occurs on the data. However, in the case of big data, data transfers of mammoth size are required. Therefore, the overheads involved are immense. Moreover, this system is not scalable.
3. The lack of sufficient processing ability forces reliable and valuable data to die its death.

Hadoop provides scalable solutions for the storage and processing of big data. In the process, it solves all three problems.

- 100% of the data is available for analysis in this case. All the data is stored on a cluster of computers and can be accessed and used for analysis. Therefore, data remains alive forever.
- The growing data situation does not affect the solution presented by Hadoop for the simple reason that the increasing data can be saved on the cluster without a possibility of lack of storage space. Therefore, Hadoop presents a scalable solution for the storage and processing of data.

- Lastly, Hadoop enables data exploration and advanced analytics because the whole heap of data is now available to analytics tools and systems, which can be churned for advanced analytics.

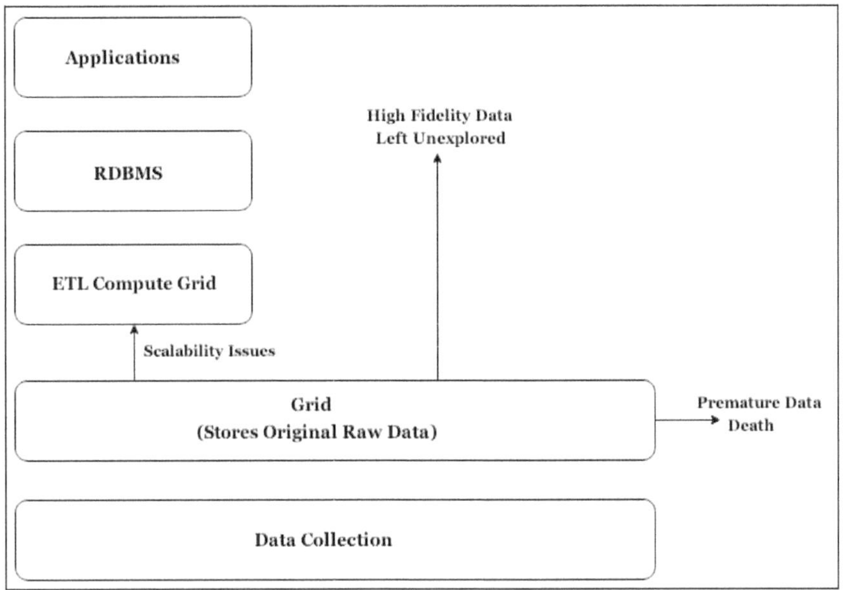

Fig. 1.4 Problems with Existing Architectures

A distributed filesystem can fasten storage and processing capabilities considerably. The improved processing speed can be explained with the help of an example. Let us consider an example where 1TB data needs to be read. If there is one machine with 4 I/O channels and each channel has a speed of transfer of 100 MB/s, then this machine will take 1024 GB/(100*4) = 43 minutes to read 1 TB data. On the other hand, if you use 10 machines, this job can be done in 43/10 = 4.3 minutes. This solution can be scaled to any level. For instance, you may choose to have 100 machines, and the time required to read this data, in that case, would be 43/100 = .43 minutes. Distributed storage and computing reduce the processing time significantly.

1.6 KEY CHARACTERISTICS OF HADOOP

Hadoop allows distributed processing of large datasets across clusters of commodity computers using a simple programming model (MapReduce). It is an Open Source Data Management System for storage (HDFS) and distributed processing (MapReduce). One of the key features of Hadoop is its ability to scale-out storage and processing ability.

If you increase the number of machines in the cluster, the storage and processing ability also correspondingly increase. Therefore, Hadoop allows horizontal scalability (more machines means better performance). Besides this, Hadoop allows you to write your own programs like graph processing algorithms over and above the base framework. Some of the key characteristics of Hadoop can be summarized as follows –

1. Economical
   A cluster of commodity computers can be provided to improve the system's storage ability and processing potential. Cluster/ Cloud computing provides you with an economical solution to the infrastructure availability problem.
2. Scalable
   Any amount of data can be stored and processed. With Hadoop, all you need to do is add more machines.
3. Reliable
   Hadoop has a default replication factor of 3. Therefore, 3 copies of data are stored, and even if one of the machines goes down, the data will be available on the other 2 machines. Another aspect of Hadoop that makes it all the more reliable is that data is stored as blocks, and each of these blocks is replicated 3 times. Therefore, reliability is ensured at the block level and not at the file level.
   Example for replication –
   Data = 1 TB or 1048576 Bytes
   Block Size for Hadoop 2.0 = 128 MB
   Number of blocks = 8192 or ~8K blocks

Each block is replicated thrice and saved on three different machines.

Block 1: [128] [128] [128]

Block 2: [128] [128] [128]

Block 3: [128] [128] [128]

Block 4: [128] [128] [128].

...

Block n or 8192: [128] [128] [128]

Please note that changing the value of the corresponding parameter in the config. file can change the replication factor.

4. Flexible

   If you need to add or remove a machine, you do not need to bring the cluster down for the operation. Adding and removing data are possible operations, and none of them disturb the cluster in any way.

1.7 KEY DIFFERENCES BETWEEN RDBMS AND HADOOP

The main differences between Hadoop and RDBMS are summarized in Table 1.1.

Table 1.1 Differences Between RDBMS and Hadoop

S. No.	Hadoop	RDBMS
1.	Multi-structured and unstructured data can be handled.	Only structured data is handled.
2.	If there are three blocks of data and program needs to be run on this data, then multiple copies of the program are created and transferred to the three machines. Therefore, data is not moved to the process. Instead, process is moved to the data. In other words, processing is coupled with data.	Data is moved to the process and the program is run. Therefore, limited or no data processing occurs.

S. No.	Hadoop	RDBMS
3.	Loosely structured governance in terms of the fact that you don't need to predefine everything. In Hadoop, you give the structure only when you have to insert data.	Governance follows standards and is structured. In other words, RDBS requires you to define a structure even before you start inserting any data.
4.	Write is faster because validation of schema is done (NULL or NOT NULL) only during reading. Therefore, Writes are faster in Hadoop.	Write takes time as schema is validated before every write. However, reads do not perform schema validation. Therefore, in this case, reads are faster.
5.	Hadoop is open source. Therefore, no license is required.	Costly because licenses are required.
6.	Open source makes the Hadoop platform extensive, complex and a growing platform. Therefore, resources may not always be available for everything.	Since it is paid, resources are pre-available.
7.	Best uses of Hadoop: processing unstructured data, data discovery and massive storage and processing.	Use cases for RDBMS: OLTP, complex ACID transactions and operational data store.

Note:

- Hadoop does not allow selective editing or deleting of data, which is its most significant limitation. Therefore, Hadoop cannot be used for OLTP-type applications.
- Hadoop is typically used for data of the order of TBs for which standard RDBMSs fail. Although it works effectively on large datasets, it can be used for small and large datasets. When working on small datasets, the overhead of working with Hadoop will make the benefits of Hadoop unimportant.

OBJECTIVE-TYPE QUESTIONS

1. Which of these sources generate big data?
   a. Stock market
   b. Social media portals
   c. Geoscience applications
   d. All of the above
2. Which of these data are classified as semi-structured data?
   a. CRM Data
   b. Audio Files
   c. Emails
   d. Text Files
3. Which of the following is not a big data characteristic as given in the IBM's 3V Model?
   a. Viability
   b. Velocity
   c. Volume
   d. Variety

SHORT ANSWER QUESTIONS

1. Differentiate between structured and semi-structured data with the help of examples?
2. Assuming the version of Hadoop to be Hadoop 2.x, calculate the number of blocks required to store 5 TB data?
3. Can Hadoop be used for storing and processing small and structured datasets?
4. Compare Hadoop's storage ability with data warehouses?

LONG ANSWER QUESTIONS

1. Describe the big data problem and elaborate on the need for Hadoop?
2. Provide five use cases of big data and possible applications of Hadoop in them?
3. Why is distributed filesystem considered an appropriate solution to the storage and processing needs of the big data problem?
4. Explain the reliability characteristic of Hadoop along with a detailed description of the mechanisms used to ensure file-level and block-level reliability?

Chapter 2

HADOOP AND HDFS ARCHITECTURE

OBJECTIVES

- Core Components of Hadoop Ecosystem
- Hadoop Functions: Data Placement, Read and Write
- Hadoop 2.x Cluster Architecture – Federation and High Availability
- Resource Management in Hadoop
- Cluster Modes
- Configuration Files

2.1 HADOOP ECOSYSTEM

The first version of Hadoop was Hadoop 1.x. Then, the improved form of this version was released as Hadoop 2.x. The two main differences between these versions were YARN's introduction and HBase's exclusion from the MapReduce framework to transform it into an independent component. Fig. 2.1 illustrates the block diagrams of Hadoop 1.0 and Hadoop 2.0 for better comparison.

2.1.1 Comparison Between Hadoop 1.x and Hadoop 2.x

The similarities and differences between Hadoop 1.x and Hadoop 2.x have been summarized in Table 2.1.

Table 2.1 Comparisons Between Hadoop 1.x and Hadoop 2.x

Function	Hadoop 1.x	Hadoop 2.x
File System for storing data	HDFS	HDFS
Data Importing Techniques	Flume for semi-structured and unstructured data and Sqoop for structured data. Sqoop allows both importing and exporting data. However, flume only allows import of data.	Flume and Sqoop
Processing	Processing of data is done using MapReduce programming model.	Processing of data is done using YARN, which supports MapReduce programming model, and other YARN frameworks like MPI or graph algorithms.
Database	HBase – SQL database (part of MapReduce framework in this Hadoop version).	HBase – SQL database (enhanced) and used on top of Hadoop. A full-fledged project in this version of Hadoop.

Function	Hadoop 1.x	Hadoop 2.x
Tools	Directly programming the MapReduce programming framework, using Java, is a complex task. Therefore, Hive and Pig Latin programming languages are used. They provide interfaces that take your programs and transform them into MapReduce programming format for execution. Benefit is simplicity!	Pig and Hive
Machine Learning	Mahout is an abstraction tool for machine learning algorithms and using this tool, you can do clustering, recommendations and classifications.	Mahout
Workflow Engine	Apache Oozie is the workflow engine that allows you to schedule workflow of your Hadoop project.	Apache Oozie

Other important points related to this topic are as follows:

- YARN in Hadoop 2.x is a more generic resource manager and enhances the ability of Hadoop.
- HCatalog is used for managing metadata in Hadoop.
- Pig Latin is used for data processing and not data analysis.
- Machine Learning with Mahout
  - It uses Hadoop at backend and allows you to create applications based on clustering, recommendations and classifications. Example: recommendations app at LinkedIn.
  - It offers ensured accuracy with large datasets used for analysis.

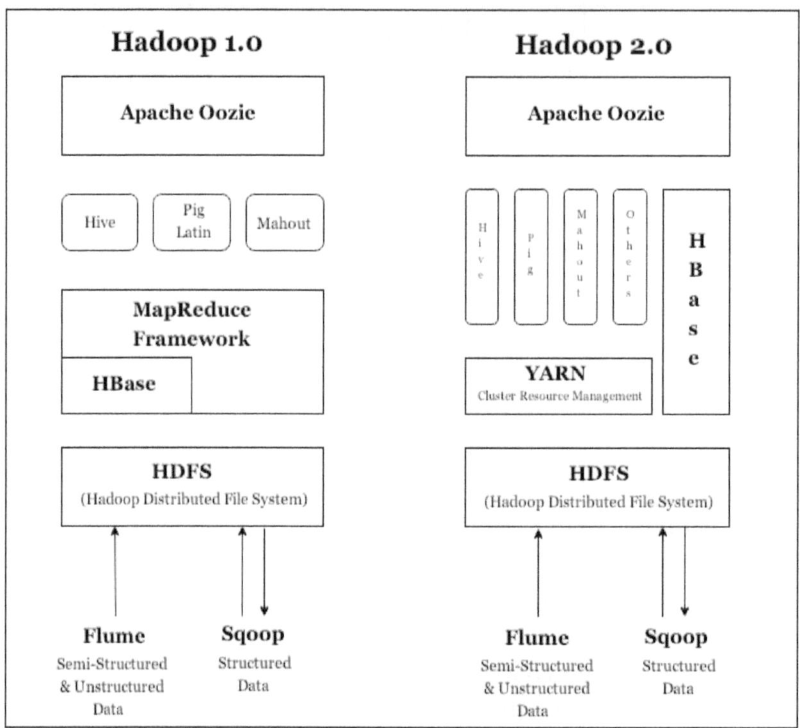

Fig. 2.1 Difference Between Hadoop 1.0 and Hadoop 2.0

2.2 CORE COMPONENTS OF HADOOP 2.X

The Hadoop Ecosystem can be broadly divided into two components, out of which one is used for storage while the other is used for processing. Firstly, data needs to be distributed and stored across a cluster of commodity computers. In order to perform this function, the storage component (HDFS) has been put in place.

Secondly, we need to read the data and process it. These functions are performed by the processing component of the Hadoop Ecosystem (YARN). Owing to the master-slave architecture of the Hadoop ecosystem, both the storage and processing components have respective master and slave daemons.

Fig. 2.2 describes the master-slave architecture of Hadoop. NameNode is the master daemon of the storage component (HDFS), while DataNode is the corresponding slave daemon. On the other hand, ResourceManager is the master daemon of the processing component (YARN), and NodeManager is the corresponding slave daemon.

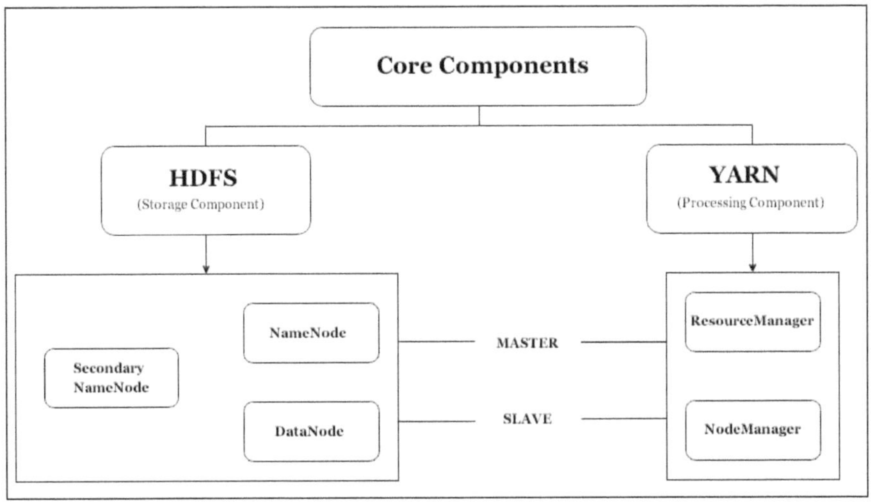

Fig. 2.2 Core Components

2.2.1 Storage Aspect of Hadoop

NameNode is the master and stores all the information about the machine and the data's whereabouts in terms of its storage locations. However, it is essential to note that NameNode only stores metadata. It maintains metadata about DataNodes in the main memory. The primary objective behind this strategy is to reduce access time, which is high for disk memory. In addition, no demand paging is required because the metadata is maintained on the main memory.

- Metadata on NameNode includes files, blocks in each file, DataNodes for each file, file attributes like replication factor and access time.
- NameNode stores transaction log, which includes deletion and creation log.

DataNode is the slave that stores the data. It takes all the read and write requests. Therefore, if there is a read or write request, then NameNode identifies the DataNode for which the request is meant, and the actual read/write happens directly between the DataNode and the client. Please note that one machine can have only one DataNode daemon on it.

Data is stored in the form of blocks. The distribution of data in blocks and their placement in the Hadoop cluster has been described below. The default block sizes for Hadoop are as follows:

Hadoop 1.x = 64 MB

Hadoop 2.x = 128 MB

In order to understand this concept, let us go back to the example previously used for replication –

Data = 1 TB or 1048576 Bytes

Block Size for Hadoop 2.0 = 128 MB

Number of blocks = 8192 or ~8K blocks

Replication factor = 3 (default)

Each block is replicated thrice and saved on three different machines.

Block 1: [128] [128] [128]

Block 2: [128] [128] [128]

Block 3: [128] [128] [128]

...

Block n or 8192: [128] [128] [128]

Placing Data blocks into the Hadoop Cluster –

Assuming there are machines: 1, 2, 3, 4, 5, 6, 7, 8, 9, 10...

Block 1: [128] -> 2 [128] -> 7 [128] -> 3

Block 2: [128] -> 5 [128] -> 3 [128] -> 8

Risk Associated with NameNode and Need for Secondary NameNode -

All the metadata lies on the NameNode, making it the single failure point. To avoid the risk associated with it, a Secondary NameNode is maintained. The Secondary NameNode connects to NameNode every hour for backup and housekeeping. In case of NameNode failure, it can be used to revive lost metadata. There also exists a concept of Standby NameNode. If the NameNode crashes in less than an hour, the Standby takes over as soon as the Active NameNode dies. This feature is an enhancement in Hadoop 2.x.

2.2.2 Processing Aspect of Hadoop

Resource Manager allocates machines by processing and identifying where the required data is residing. On the other hand, NodeManager performs data processing on the identified machines.

Convention:

The master machine has daemons for NameNode and ResourceManager, but by default, it is referred to as NameNode. On the other hand, the slave machine has daemons for DataNode and NodeManager, but by default, it is referred to as NodeManager. The configuration has been illustrated in Fig. 2.3.

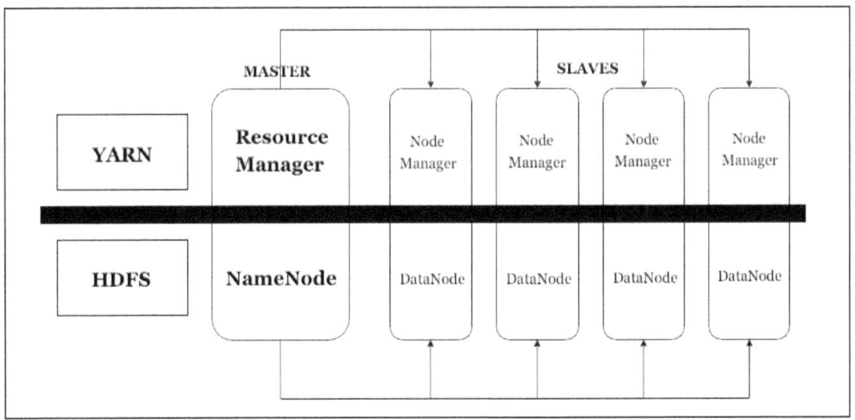

Fig. 2.3 Block Diagram of Storage and Processing Components of Hadoop

2.3 HADOOP FUNCTIONS

In order to use data on the cluster, three basic Hadoop functions need to be performed. These functions include data placement, read and write. The HDFS (storage component of Hadoop) typically has many DataNodes (slaves) that are connected to a NameNode (master). The DataNodes are arranged in the form of racks, with each rack having a few DataNodes in it. The basic HDFS architecture has been illustrated below in Fig. 2.4.

2.3.1 Placing Data

Whenever you set up a Hadoop Cluster, you must give the rack topology (or network topology). The Hadoop cluster is divided into racks, which constitute a set of machines. All the machines in the rack are connected to a switch. Now, whenever you wish to store data, the data is divided into blocks, and the NameNode decides the machines at which these blocks will be kept.

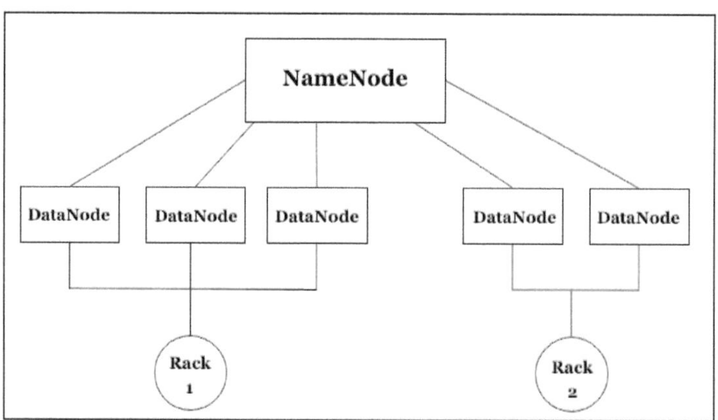

Fig. 2.4 Basic HDFS Architecture

Assuming the replication factor is 3, the NameNode will need to determine where each block's three copies will be saved. At this point, the concept of rack awareness comes into being. Whenever the NameNode chooses a machine from a rack x to store one copy of a block, it ensures that the other two block copies are stored on any rack other than x. This arrangement, in turn, ensures higher availability of data and provides rack-level reliability to the system. Even if a rack is down or the rack switch is inaccessible, the data will still be available from the other racks.

2.3.2 Reading Data

Whenever a client system needs to read data, it contacts the NameNode for metadata about where the blocks for the data are located. The client can directly connect to the DataNodes containing the required data to read it. The entire process is illustrated in Fig. 2.5.

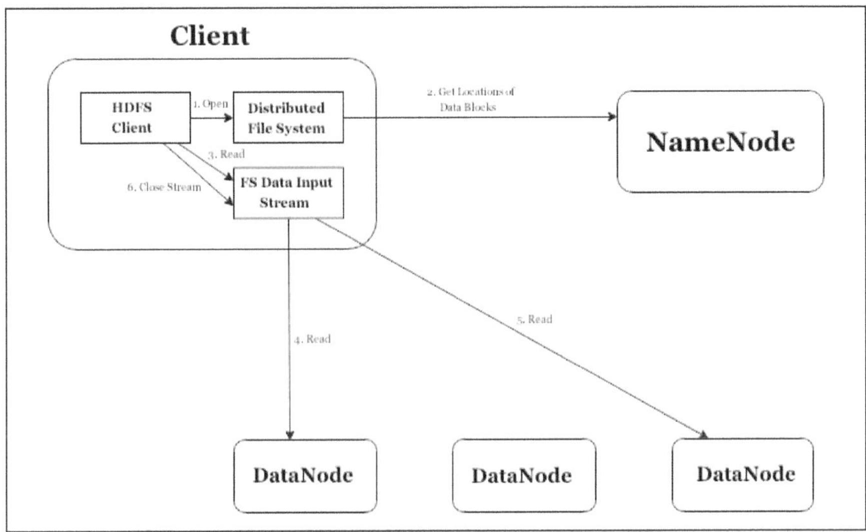

Fig. 2.5 Flow Diagram for Data Read

2.3.3 Writing Data

The client contacts the NameNode with a data write request for writing data. The NameNode allocates DataNodes for blocks. The client connects with the DataNode and writes data onto it. The DataNode returns acknowledgments after the first machine has performed data writing. Replication happens in a pipeline. The client receives an ACK after one copy has been written, and machine 1 (that has got the copy) connects with the following machine and creates a copy of the data on that machine.

The second machine contacts the third machine and creates a copy on it. The complete process has been illustrated in Fig. 2.6.

NameNode keeps carrying out a health check of machines, and if a machine seems to be going down, a copy of the data blocks present on this machine is made to another machine. Then, the other two copies can be saved on the same machine or different machines. Typically, copies are saved on two machines, which are present on the same rack, because if we save three copies on three different racks, there will be massive network overhead, which is not desirable.

If blocks are being written and a client wants to read this data, then the client can read the data up to the block that has been written. It will not have to wait until the completion of the Data Write operation.

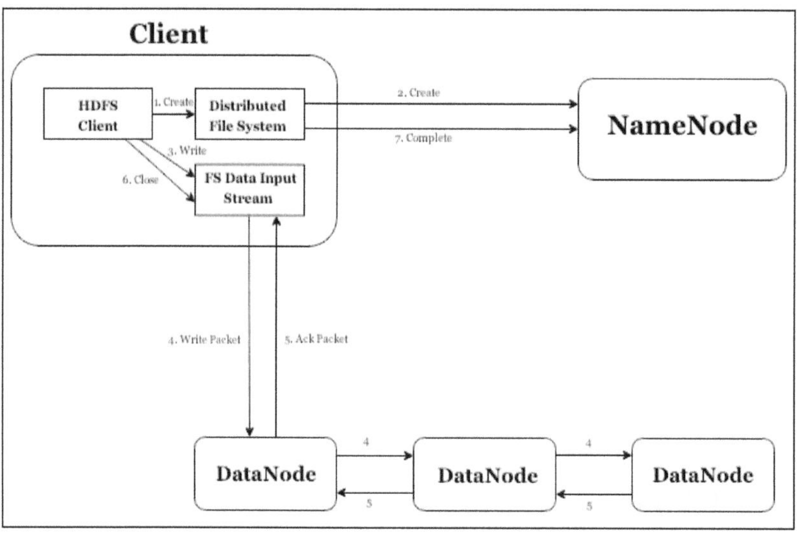

Fig. 2.6 Flow Diagram for Data Write

2.4 HADOOP 2.X CLUSTER ARCHITECTURE – FEDERATION AND AVAILABILITY

Hadoop 1.0 supports a single NameNode in a cluster, while Hadoop 2.0 supports multiple NameNodes. Moreover, in Hadoop 1.0, NameNode is the single point of failure. On the contrary, Hadoop 2.0 has a NameNode in active and passive modes. So, if the active NameNode fails, the passive NameNode can take over.

This configuration makes the system more reliable and improves the system's availability. Passive or Standby NameNode is the hot backup of the Active NameNode because the standby NameNode takes over immediately and automatically if the active NameNode fails. The NameNodes and DataNodes present in the Hadoop Federation have been shown below in Fig. 2.7.

HDFS Federation refers to the multiple NameNode support in clusters. This feature allows and supports the high availability of Hadoop 2.x. The active NameNode manages the DataNodes while the passive or standby NameNode keeps reading shared edit logs and updates its namespace accordingly. As soon as the active NameNode dies, the passive NameNode immediately takes over. In this context, the secondary NameNode keeps a backup of the active NameNode.

Shared edit logs are the point of communication between the active and standby NameNodes. The difference between standby and secondary NameNode is that the switching from active to passive NameNode upon Active NameNode failure is automatic. However, in order to switch to the usage of secondary NameNode, manual intervention is required.

The standby NameNode does not need to contact the secondary NameNode as it has all the information it needs to get started. Given this, the concept of secondary NameNode becomes irrelevant to the federation, considering that many people do not even configure Secondary NameNode.

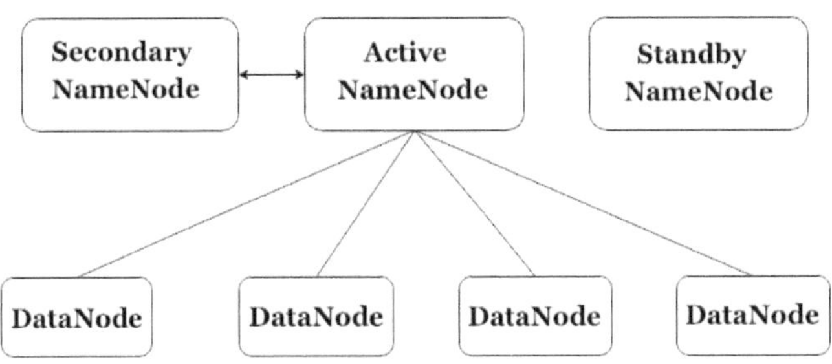

Fig. 2.7 Cluster Architecture of Hadoop 2.x

2.4.1 Role of Shared Edit Logs

The active NameNode writes to the Shared Edit Logs, and the Standby keeps reading these logs to update itself. The write access is given to only one Node at a time, which is enabled using the fencing technique. Hadoop 2.x allows the use of multiple NameNodes. Therefore, for every NameNode, a connected standby NameNode is also created.

2.4.2 Fencing

A memory barrier, also known as a membar, memory fence, or fence instruction, is a type of barrier instruction that causes a central processing unit (CPU) or compiler to enforce an ordering constraint on memory operations issued before and after the barrier instruction. It typically means that execution of the operations issued prior to the barrier is guaranteed before the operations issued.

2.5 RESOURCE MANAGEMENT IN HADOOP 2.X

The function of ResourceManager is to allocate resources based on data availability. On the other hand, the function of NodeManager is to perform actual processing. Therefore, ResourceManager has two components, Scheduler and ApplicationsManager (AsM). The scheduler performs the scheduling of resources. However, the NodeManager has two components, namely, Container and ApplicationMaster. ApplicationsManager manages all the applications that are running in the cluster.

ApplicationMaster manages the lifecycle of applications. For each application, there is an AppMaster. The job of the AppMaster is to negotiate the resources required by the application with the ResourceManager. Then, based on the case put up by the AppMaster, the ResourceManager allocates resources. In other words, the job of the ResourceManager is to allocate resources while the whole process of resource allocation is overlooked and managed by the AppMaster.

The ApplicationMaster also performs other functions like restarting a resource on another machine or requesting some new resources. Upon the request put up by the ApplicationMaster, the ResourceManager allocates resources to the NodeManager in the form of containers, which the NodeManager then uses to perform the required processing. Fig. 2.8 illustrates the essential components of YARN. Processing in the Hadoop ecosystem is performed by YARN, which stands for 'Yet Another Resource Negotiator.'

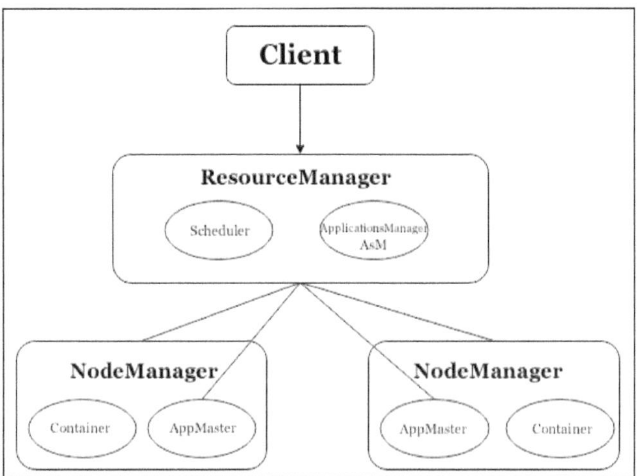

Fig. 2.8 Basic Components of YARN

2.5.1 The Negotiation Process

1. Whenever an application starts, the ResourceManager creates the AppMaster for the application, which determines the resources required by the application and informs the same to the ResourceManager.
2. Depending on the job's priority, which is where the scheduler comes into play, the resources are allocated by the ResourceManager to the concerned NodeManager in the form of containers.
3. The NodeManager makes use of the container to execute the assigned job.

2.5.2 Advantages of the YARN Architecture

Hadoop 1.x had JobTracker, responsible for submitting and tracking jobs, and TaskTracker. HDFS-HA (High Availability) was developed to overcome one of the most significant disadvantages of Hadoop 1.0: Single Point of Failure. In addition, YARN Resource Manager was developed to overcome the following disadvantages of JobTracker in Hadoop 1.0:

1. Too much burden on JobTracker
2. Only one version can be run in Classic MapReduce.

Key advantages of using YARN Architecture as part of the Hadoop ecosystem include –

1. Scalability
2. Flexibility

Other applications like graph processing can also be now performed using Hadoop.

2.5.3 YARN: Moving Beyond MapReduce

YARN improves the functionality and ability of Hadoop. Most of the work done in this area is performed by Hortonworks. You can have a range of jobs running on MapReduce now. These include batch processing (MapReduce), streaming (Storm), and graph processing (Giraph) jobs, in addition to several others.

Multi-tenancy Capacity Scheduler is one of the most critical components of YARN. Some important points regarding this scheduler include –

1. Jobs are organized into queues, and queues follow FIFO scheduling.
2. Data locality-aware scheduling takes place.
3. Two main features include multi-tenancy (set limit to prevent over-utilization of resources by a single application) and capacity

guarantee (a fraction of the total available capacity allocated to each queue).

4. Other features include security, elasticity, operability, and resource-based scheduling.

2.6 CLUSTER MODES

Hadoop can operate in one of the following cluster modes:

- Standalone or Local Mode
  The key features of this mode include –
  - Single JVM
  - No daemons
  - No DFS
  - Can be used during development for testing logic without the need to transfer data to and from the HDFS.
  - It is similar to a simulation mode.
- Pseudo-Distributed Mode
  - Daemons run on the local machine.
  - VM uses pseudo-distributed mode.
- Fully-Distributed Mode
  - Daemons run on a cluster of machines.

Cluster is a set of machines and the organization of these machines in the cluster is determined by rack topology.

2.7 CONFIGURATION FILES

There are several tasks that require access to configuration files and editing of the same. One such example is changing the replication factor. Table 2.2 provides some common configuration files along with the functions they monitor and control.

Table. 2.2 Different Configuration Files

Filename	Includes
hadoop-env.sh	Environment variables
core-site.xml	Config settings common to HDFS and MapReduce like I/O settings
hdfs-site.xml	HDFS related configuration settings (this is where the replication factor is also set), includes settings related to NameNodes and DataNodes
mapred-site.xml	MapReduce applications – related configuration settings
yarn-site.xml	YARN – related config settings and includes settings related to NodeManager and ResourceManager
Masters	List of machines acting as secondary NameNode, entered one item per line
Slaves	List of machines running as slaves (i.e. have daemons, NodeManager and DataNode running on them), entered one item per line

It is important to note that the XML files have these values in the form of key-value pairs. They assume default values upon installation and can be edited later on, on a requirement basis. Some key points to remember are –

- Adding and removing machines do not require a restart of the cluster.
- The startup and shutdown commands use two files, masters and slaves.
- Every node has the config files. The master file is empty for a worker node because it cannot have any secondary NameNode and the slaves' file has its IP address.

OBJECTIVE-TYPE QUESTIONS

1. Which of these components is a part of Hadoop 2.x, but is missing in Hadoop 1.x?

   a. Oozie
   b. YARN
   c. MapReduce Framework
   d. HDFS

2. Which Data Loading tool is used for importing semi-structured and unstructured data?

   a. Flume
   b. Sqoop
   c. Command Line Import
   d. None of the above

3. Identify the master daemon(s) from among the following –

   a. NameNode
   b. DataNode
   c. ResourceManager
   d. Both a and c

SHORT ANSWER QUESTIONS

1. Describe the key functions of NameNode and DataNode? Explicitly specify the data stored on the same.
2. Distinguish between Secondary NameNode and Standby NameNode? Explain how each of these communicates with the active NameNode.
3. How does Hadoop 2.x improves the shortcomings of Hadoop 2.0?
4. Does master and slave daemons exist in the Pseudo-distributed cluster mode?
5. In the standalone or Pseudo-distributed mode of operation, what will be the contents of the masters and slaves config files?

LONG ANSWER QUESTIONS

1. Describe the different components of the Hadoop Ecosystem, elaborating on the function of each of the components? Also, state the key differences between Hadoop 1.x and Hadoop 2.x?
2. How does replication happen inside the Hadoop ecosystem? Can replication factor be changed?
3. Is the topology and configuration of racks default or user-defined? Also, explain how the rack awareness concept improves the reliability of the Hadoop ecosystem?

Chapter 3

BASICS OF MAPREDUCE FRAMEWORK

OBJECTIVES

- Introduction to MapReduce Programming Paradigm
- Comparison of Traditional Method with MapReduce
- Implementing Logic in MapReduce
- MapReduce Architecture
- Job Submission Flow in MapReduce

3.1 MAPREDUCE PROGRAMMING PARADIGM

MapReduce Framework is a programming paradigm for the development of distributed applications. *Hadoop* is a distributed framework that implements the MapReduce programming paradigm to enable the processing of large datasets. In order to help you relate to real-world problems that can be solved using the MapReduce programming paradigm, let us take an example. Determination of maximum temperature recorded in a year is one of the simplest use-cases of big data analytics. The weather data for the whole year needs to be scanned for this purpose and processed to determine the required outcome.

3.2 TRADITIONAL WAY OF PROCESSING LARGE DATA

In order to illustrate the traditional form of data processing, let us consider an example where we need to observe if a particular error has occurred in any of the system applications or components. For this, all the log files need to be scanned for error statements.

In Linux, the grep command is used for pattern matching. Therefore, the grep command is run on the log files. When a statement matching the given error statement is found, the corresponding result is outputted. However, in this approach, since there is a single grep process that scans all log files of the system, it will take much time to scan all the log files in the system.

This data can be split into sections to fasten processing, and grep can be run on each data split. The outputs are then aggregated to form results. The challenges involved in using the traditional system include:

1. There is a need for a mechanism that can split data.
2. There is a need for a mechanism to aggregate the results.

3.3 THE MAPREDUCE APPROACH

From the last approach, three main phases can be identified. These phases include splitting data, processing splits, and aggregating results. In order to see how MapReduce does this, the data splitting process needs to be understood. Whenever data is stored in HDFS, the storage is done in blocks. Therefore, data is automatically split. Therefore, any MapReduce program is executed in two phases – Map and Reduce. During the first phase, data is analyzed. On the other hand, data analysis results are aggregated and summarized during the second phase.

Advantages of using MapReduce Framework include –

1. Processing is taken to data
2. Data is processed in parallel, improving system performance

The process is moved to data instead of moving the data to the process. Transferring data is a challenge in the big data scenario because the volume of this data is enormous. This approach reduces the need to transfer vast amounts of data across the cluster, reducing network transfer overhead. Additionally, this approach improves the scalability of the system. No matter how big the data gets, the overhead for transfer remains the same because we are no longer transferring data.

One of the most critical tasks in the execution of the MapReduce code is allotment of processor, which may take place in one of the three ways –

- Case I –
  Whenever data needs to be processed, the ResourceManager will allot a map task to the machine with the block of data that needs to be processed. This use case is the best-case scenario.
- Case II –
  There may be a situation where no processor may be available on the machine. The ResourceManager will allocate a machine on the same rack in such a case. Slight movement of data may be required in this case.
- Case III –
  The worst-case scenario, and perhaps a rare scenario, is that no machine on the same rack is available. Therefore, a machine on a different rack may need to be assigned. In case the data and map task assigned for it is not on the same machine, data will need to be transferred to the machine, which has been assigned for processing. This transfer is more straightforward within the same rack and incurs significantly lesser overhead. On the other hand, transferring data between racks is costly and involves much overhead. The workflow in the case of MapReduce programming is as follows –
  1. Assuming that data resides on a relational database, data will be imported into HDFS using Sqoop, a popular data loading technique.
  2. The MapReduce program reads the data from the HDFS.
  3. The Map logic is applied to the imported data, and the output of this processing is fed as input to the Reduce program logic.

The output generated from the Reduce logic is the final output of the MapReduce program.

This output is saved back to the HDFS in a CSV file.

3.4 MAPREDUCE VS TRADITIONAL PROGRAMMING APPROACHES

Both approaches solve the same set of problems. However, MapReduce provides much better performance. In this section, we shall see how the same problem is solved using both these approaches. In order to help you understand better, let us take an example. Assuming that you have the following dataset and the problem is to count the number of occurrences of each word in the file.

3.4.1 Sample File

abc efg ijk lmn
abc efg ijk lmn
abc efg ijk lmn
abc efg ijk lmn
abc efg ijk lmn
abc efg ijk lmn

3.4.2 Traditional Approach

The first approach is to set 4 variables to calculate the frequency of a word present in the file. The data is processed line by line, and the variable counter is incremented accordingly.

By the end of processing, the values of the four counter variables would be –

counter_abc = 6
counter_efg = 6
counter_ijk = 6
counter_lmn = 6

3.4.3 MapReduce Approach

Using this approach, we have a process to deal with each of the lines of data (P1, P2, P3, and P4 for each of the lines), and each process increments the four variable counters based on the occurrences of each of the words. By the end of processing, the values of the four counter variables for each of the processes will be as follows –

P1 =>	*P2 =>*	*P3 =>*
counter_abc = 1	*counter_abc = 1*	*counter_abc = 1*
counter_efg = 1	*counter_efg = 1*	*counter_efg = 1*
counter_ijk = 1	*counter_ijk = 1*	*counter_ijk = 1*
counter_lmn = 1	*counter_lmn = 1*	*counter_lmn = 1*

P4 =>	*P5 =>*	*P6 =>*
counter_abc = 1	*counter_abc = 1*	*counter_abc = 1*
counter_efg = 1	*counter_efg = 1*	*counter_efg = 1*
counter_ijk = 1	*counter_ijk = 1*	*counter_ijk = 1*
counter_lmn = 1	*counter_lmn = 1*	*counter_lmn = 1*

In order to determine the final result, these preliminary results need to be aggregated or reduced. The final output will look like –

counter_abc = 6
counter_efg = 6
counter_ijk = 6
counter_lmn = 6

3.4.4 Comparison of Two Approaches

Approach 1 is a sequential form of processing, but approach 2 is a simulation of parallel processing. The problem with the traditional approach is that if the processor fails at any step, the whole process will come to a halt, and the whole of the remaining task will be performed only after the processor has been fixed.

On the other hand, in the MapReduce approach, if any of the six processors fails, the rest will perform the required tasks. Whenever the failed processor is fixed, it can perform its remaining work and send it to the reducer. As a result, the MapReduce approach handles failure more gracefully.

3.5 MAPREDUCE IMPLEMENTATION

The algorithm for implementing the word count example is given below.

```
/*Perform processing of data*/
Mapper (filename, file-contents)
        for each word in file-contents
        output (word, 1)
/*Aggregate results*/
Reducer (word, values) // abc [1, 1, 1, 1, 1, 1]
        sum = 0
        for each value in values
        sum = sum + value
        output (word, sum) // abc 6
```

Java Implementation for the algorithm is as follows –

Filename: WordCount.java

```
import java.io.IOException;
import java.util.StringTokenizer;
import org.apache.hadoop.io.IntWritable;
import org.apache.hadoop.io.LongWritable;
import org.apache.hadoop.io.Text;
import org.apache.hadoop.mapreduce.Mapper;
import org.apache.hadoop.mapreduce.Reducer;
import org.apache.hadoop.conf.Configuration;
import org.apache.hadoop.mapreduce.Job;
import org.apache.hadoop.mapreduce.lib.input.TextInputFormat;
import org.apache.hadoop.mapreduce.lib.output.TextOutputFormat;
import org.apache.hadoop.mapreduce.lib.input.FileInputFormat;
```

```
import org.apache.hadoop.mapreduce.lib.output.FileOutputFormat;
import org.apache.hadoop.fs.Path;

public class WordCount {
    public static class Map extends
    Mapper<LongWritable, Text, Text,IntWritable>{
        public void map(LongWritable key, Text value,
                Context context)
                throws IOException,InterruptedException {
            String line = value.toString();
            StringTokenizer tokenizer = new StringTokenizer(line);
            while (tokenizer.hasMoreTokens()) {
                value.set(tokenizer.nextToken());
                context.write(value, new IntWritable(1));
            }
        }
    }

    public static class Reduce extends
    Reducer<Text,IntWritable, Text,IntWritable>{
        public void reduce(Text key, Iterable<IntWritable> values,
                Context context)
                throws IOException,InterruptedException {
            int sum=0;
            for(IntWritable x: values)
            {
                sum+=x.get();
            }
            context.write(key, new IntWritable(sum));
        }
    }
```

```
    public static void main(String[] args) throws Exception {
        Configuration conf= new Configuration();
        Job job = new Job(conf,"mywc");
        job.setJarByClass(WordCount.class);
        job.setMapperClass(Map.class);
        job.setReducerClass(Reduce.class);
        job.setOutputKeyClass(Text.class);
        job.setOutputValueClass(IntWritable.class);
        job.setInputFormatClass(TextInputFormat.class);
        job.setOutputFormatClass(TextOutputFormat.class);
        Path outputPath = new Path(args[1]);

    //Configuring the input/output path from the filesystem into the job
     FileInputFormat.addInputPath(job, new Path(args[0]));
     FileOutputFormat.setOutputPath(job, new Path(args[1]));

    //deleting the output path automatically from HDFS so that we don't have
    delete it explicitly
        outputPath.getFileSystem(conf).delete(outputPath);

    //exiting the job only if the flag value becomes false
        System.exit(job.waitForCompletion(true) ? 0 : 1);
    }
}
```

Mapper runs on individual systems. The reducer may also run as instances on multiple machines. Please note that each line of the file contents is used as an independent dataset.

3.6 MAPREDUCE ARCHITECTURE

The MapReduce architecture consists of three main components namely client, NameNode and DataNodes. Their functions along with the functions of their sub-components are illustrated in Fig. 3.1 and are as follows –

- Client
  The client submits a job to the MapReduce framework and typically contacts the NameNode with a request.
- NameNode
  - ResourceManager (RM)
    The ResourceManager performs cluster-level management of resources.
  - Job History Server
    This component maintains a log of MapReduce jobs submitted to the framework after the ApplicationMaster has terminated its execution.
- DataNode
  - NodeManager (NM)
    NodeManager is the slave component of the processing system. It monitors the resources available on the DataNode and provides working status of the node to the ResourceManager.
  - Container
    Upon command from the RM, NM allocates a chunk of the resources available on the DataNode to the application in the form of a container.
  - ApplicationMaster (AM)
    For every application submitted to the system, a dedicated AM is created. AM assesses the requirements of the task and negotiates resources for it from RM. On grant of request, NM grants the resources to AM. NM starts the tasks while AM monitors the status of the tasks. Moreover, the statuses of the tasks are reported by the AM to RM and Client. Lastly, AM dies immediately after the application terminates.

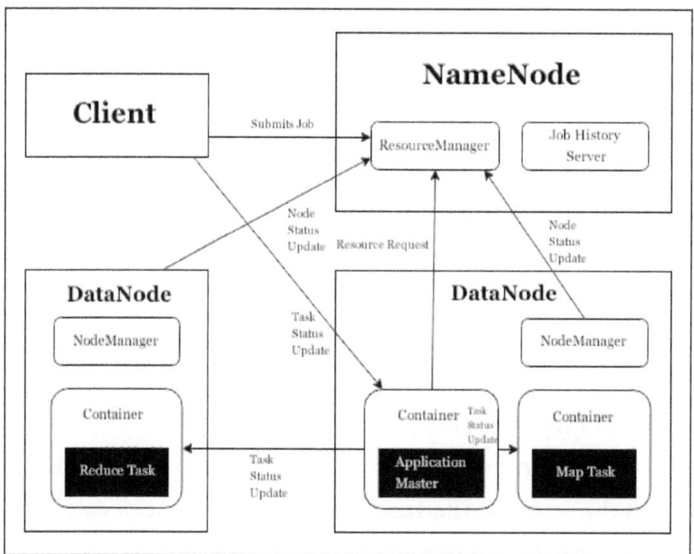

Fig. 3.1 MapReduce Architecture

3.6.1 Application Execution Workflow

The steps involved in the execution of an application are as follows –

1. Client submits a job to RM.
2. RM initiates AM and runs it in any one of the data nodes.
3. AM registers itself with RM.
4. AM analyses resource requirements and sends the same to RM.
5. RM assigns resources and notifies the same to AM.
6. AM notifies NM about the resource allocation.
7. NM conducts and manages the execution of the concerned application.
8. Client polls AM for application status and AM contacts the containers to give status update.
9. Once the application is complete, AM unregisters itself.

The block diagram for this process is given Fig. 3.2. The flow diagram is given in Fig. 3.3 for better understanding of the communication between different components of the MapReduce architecture.

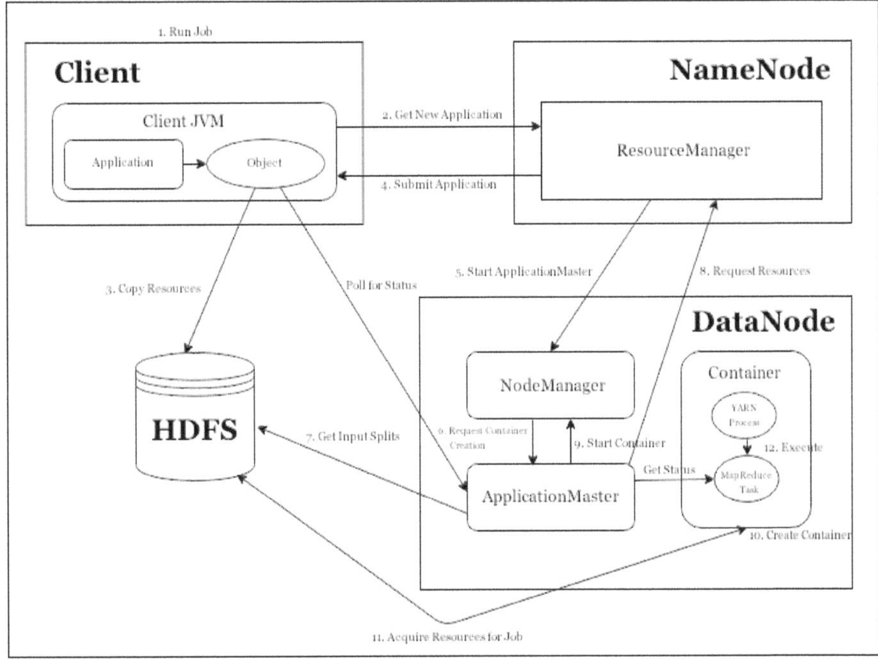

Fig. 3.2 Execution Workflow

Both containers and ApplicationMasters exist on DataNodes. However, the container allotted to an ApplicationMaster may not exist on the same DataNode as the ApplicationMaster. For example, if there are two applications, there will be two ApplicationMasters, and the containers for these two AMs may co-exist on the same DataNode. Moreover, ApplicationsManager, a sub-component of ResourceManager, monitors all the ApplicationMasters that are alive on the system. The execution assembly for YARN is illustrated in Fig. 3.4.

Please note that the JobTracker functionality in Hadoop 1.x has been replaced by YARN in Hadoop 2.x. The two components of YARN that take up the responsibilities of JobTracker are (1) Resource Manager and (2) Application Master. These two components take care of (1) resource management and job scheduling and (2) monitoring of applications.

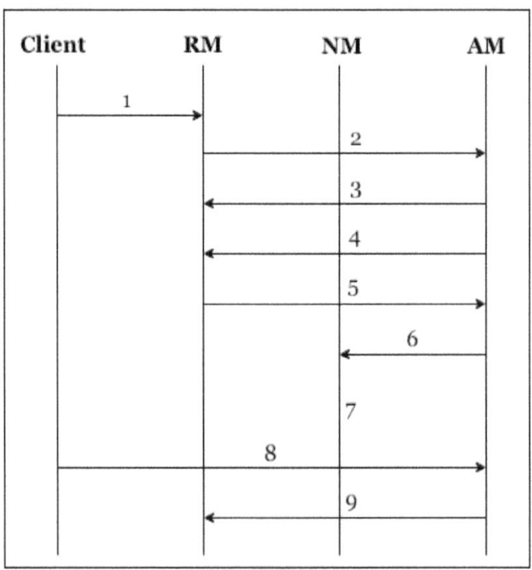

Fig. 3.3 Flow Diagram of Application Execution Workflow

3.6.2 Processes Involved

The processes involved in the execution of a MapReduce task are –

1. Input Splitting
   This process splits the dataset. The output of this process appears in the form of key-value pairs.
   Example:
   If we take the wordcount example, data is split on the basis of newline characters and the output of this process is each line.
2. Mapping
   This step performs the required processing. The output of this process appears in the form of a list of key-value pairs.
   Example:
   After the completion of map tasks, we will have a list of key-value pairs. For example, (List (K2, V2)) contains key-value pairs for all the lines.
3. Shuffling

This process is responsible for moving data from mapper to reducer. The logic used for shuffling data is called partitioner logic. Therefore, partitioner is the component that performs shuffling. The main objective of this process is to reshuffle results for the convenience of the reducer.

Example:

In order to make reduction easier, the list of key-value pairs for all the lines are arranged in such a way that we have key-value pairs in the form (key, list of values) or K2, List (V2).

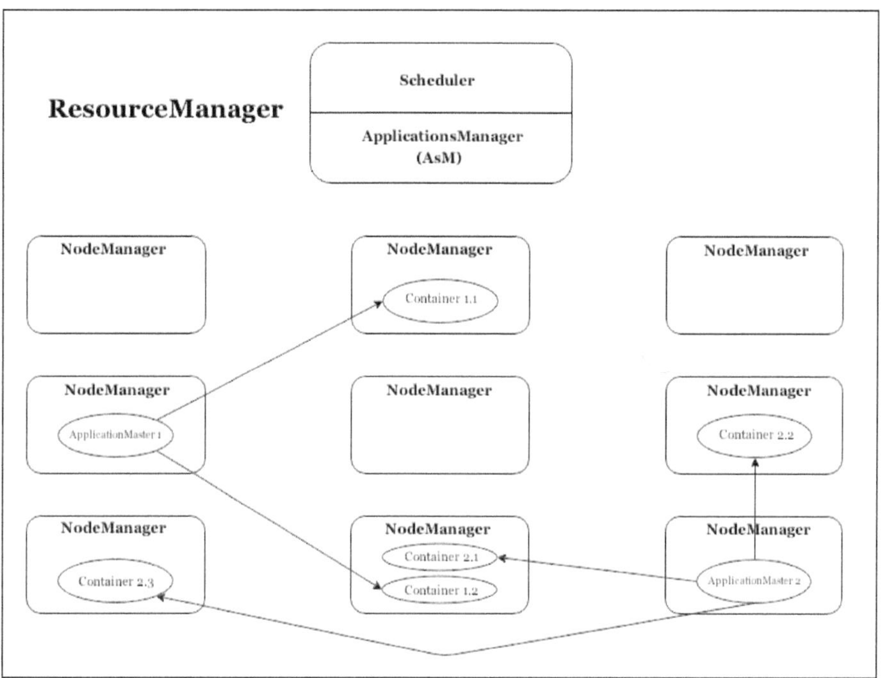

Fig. 3.4 YARN Execution Assembly

4. Reducing

   This process aggregates results. The output of this process appears in the form of key-value pairs.

   Example:

   As part of the reduction task, the list of values, corresponding to every key, are added. Therefore, after the completion of reduction tasks, we will have key-value pairs in the form (key, result value) or (K3, V3).

5. Output
   The final process presents the result to the user. The output of this process appears in the form of key-value pairs.
   Example:
   The final output is a list of key-value pairs in the form (word or key, sum of values) or list (K3, V3).

To simplify the concept, let us take a sample file and execute all the processes individually on it. Assume that the contents of the sample file are as follows –

this is my lab
my lab is wonderful
this is a wonderful lab

The outputs corresponding to each process will be as follows –

1. Input Splitting -
   Line 1: this is my lab
   Line 2: my lab is wonderful
   Line 3: this is a wonderful lab
2. Mapping -
   Mapper 1:
     (this, 1)
     (is, 1)
     (my, 1)
     (lab, 1)
   Mapper 2:
     (my, 1)
     (lab, 1)
     (is, 1)
     (wonderful, 1)
   Mapper 3:
     (this, 1)

(is, 1)
(a, 1)
(wonderful, 1)
(lab, 1)

3. Shuffling -
   (this, 1)
   (this, 1)
   (is, 1)
   (is, 1)
   (is, 1)
   (my, 1)
   (my, 1)
   (lab, 1)
   (lab, 1)
   (lab, 1)
   (wonderful, 1)
   (wonderful, 1)
   (a, 1)
4. Reducing -
   (this, 2)
   (is, 3)
   (my, 2)
   (lab, 3)
   (wonderful, 2)
   (a, 1)
5. Output -

this	2
is	3
my	2
lab	3
wonderful	2
a	1

The input and output formats for the mapper and reducer are as follows –

- Input for Mapper – (key, value)
- Output for Mapper list – (key, value)
- Input for Reducer – (key, list(value))
- Output for Reducer list – (key, value)

3.6.3 Job Submission Flow in MapReduce

The series of steps involved in job submission are as follows –

1. Data is given to the Hadoop cluster. The cluster automatically splits the data and saves it onto different cluster machines.
2. The mapper logic defines logical splits, and for each logical split, a mapper task is created.
3. The mapper output is available in the form of (key, value) pairs. This value is intermediate data of the process.
4. This data is then given to the reducers. It is important to note that the number of reducers and mappers may or may not be the same. For example, the number of reducers may be lower than the number of mappers. The mapper output is given to which reducer is determined by the partitioner logic (discussed in detail in the next chapter). However, all the intermediate data for a particular key also go to the same reducer. Therefore, it can be inferred that a reducer may be processing more than one key.
5. Transferring data from the mapper to the reducer requires data exchange between nodes. This process is called Shuffling, which is the only point where communication and data exchange occurs between nodes (communication between mapper and reducer). Map and Reduce tasks are isolated and do not communicate or exchange data at any level to avoid the complexities that may arise due to the implementation of techniques for locking and synchronization.

When the data is inputted into the Hadoop cluster, it automatically splits among different machines of the clusters. Then, the MapReduce job is written and submitted. Depending on the number of blocks, mappers are created, which run on top of the cluster's stored data. Given the number of reducer tasks, reduction and aggregation are subsequently performed.

OBJECTIVE-TYPE QUESTIONS

1. Which of these is advantage(s) of using MapReduce approach?
   a. Processing taken to data
   b. Processing takes place in parallel
   c. Improved system performance
   d. All of the above
2. Which of these components is responsible for aggregation of data?
   a. Mapper
   b. Reducer
   c. Partitioner
   d. None of the above
3. Which of the following components monitors ApplicationMasters running on the system?
   a. NodeManager
   b. JobHistoryServer
   c. ApplicationsManager
   d. None of the above

SHORT ANSWER QUESTIONS

1. Name the components with which the client directly communicates. Also mention the scenarios under which such communication occurs?
2. What is the function of shuffling? Explain with the help of examples.

3. Explain how the use of MapReduce programming approach improves system performance in comparison to the same achieved by traditional approach?
4. Explain the different scenarios of processor allotment? Which of the scenarios manifest highest system overhead and why?

LONG ANSWER QUESTIONS

1. Explain the traditional and MapReduce approaches? Also elaborate on how the approaches work with the help of an example?
2. List the different tasks performed by ApplicationMaster? Does the ApplicationMaster initiate job execution?

Chapter 4

ADVANCED CONCEPTS IN MAPREDUCE PROGRAMMING

OBJECTIVES

- Input Splits
- Combiner and Partitioner
- Map and Reduce Side Joins
- Distributed Cache Concept
- Counters for Generating Custom Metrics
- Input Formats
- MRUnit Testing Framework

4.1 INPUT SPLITS IN MAPREDUCE

Input split is a block of data that mappers take as input. However, input split (on which mappers work) and block (where data resides) are two different concepts. When data is stored in the Hadoop cluster, data is split and saved onto different machines in the form of blocks (the default block size is 128 MB).

Therefore, data is converted into blocks based on allowable HDFS block size and then physically saved onto different machines. However, when the data needs to be processed, data will be read in the form of logical splits. For instance, let us take the wordcount example with data as follows –

name1 name2 name3 namex name5
name1 name2 name3 namex name5
name1 name2 name3 namex name5
name1 name2 name3 namex name5 name3
name1 name2 name3 namex name5
name1 name2 name3 namex name5
name1 name2 name3 namex name5
name1 name2 name3 namex name5

The mapper logic splits data on the condition that a newline character has occurred in the dataset given above. Therefore, for line 4, the split occurs after name3 and not after name5. In such a scenario, the case may be such that one block may have data till name5, and name3 may have been saved in another block. However, data will make sense only if the logical split is taken into account. To solve this conflict, the mapper considers data in input splits even if data spans multiple physical blocks.

Please note that textInputFormat automatically takes in lines that terminate with a newline in the Java program.

4.2 PARTITIONER

The Partitioner logic determines which mapper needs to send its output to which reducer. Then, based on the partitioner logic, the shuffling process takes place. In other words, the partitioner logic determines which mapper output needs to go to which reducer for further processing. It is primarily a part of the shuffling logic and is implemented by the framework. However, a custom partitioner may also be given.

If no custom partitioning logic is given, the system applies default partitioning, also called hash partitioning. The logic behind this partitioning is that all the values for the same key will come to one reducer. Therefore, the system uses default partitioning if the client defines no custom partitioning. On the other hand, in the case of custom partitioning, the client can define the number of reduce tasks that need to be run.

In order to explain this concept, let us take an example. Let the number of reducers be 3 [0, 1, 2]. For every key, <key> % 3 <number of reducers> is calculated. The value of this computation will lie between 0 and (n-1), where n is the number of reducers allowed. This value will be the same if the key is the same. Therefore, the corresponding key-value pair is transferred to the reducer number corresponding to the value computed. For the example given above, modulo value for any key will lie between 0 and 2.

abc % 3 -> 1 *//given to reducer 1*
def % 3 -> 2 *//given to reducer 2*
bcd % 3 -> 1 *//given to reducer 1*
xyz % 3 -> 0 *//given to reducer 0*

Please note that hash-modulo is one of the hashing algorithms. Some other algorithms may also be used.

4.3 COMBINER

A *combiner* is a mini-reducer, which performs initial aggregation or summarization of data at the mapper level. Therefore, the number of combiners is the same as the number of mappers. The output of this mini-reducer is given to the reducer. Therefore, the traffic/overload transferred to the reducer will be comparatively less. It would not be wrong to say that combiner is a local reducer for each mapper. Consider the example of two blocks with the following characters.

Block 1 –

B
D
C
B
C
A

Block 2 –

A
C
G
C
B
B

Combiner is actually a block-level reducer. In the absence of combiner, the mapper output for the two blocks would be as follows:

Mapper 1 Output –

(B, 1)
(D, 1)
(C, 1)
(B, 1)
(C, 1)
(A, 1)

Mapper 2 Output –

(A, 1)
(C, 1)
(G, 1)
(C, 1)
(B, 1)
(B, 1)

The output of the mappers goes into the shuffling process to yield –

(A, [1, 1])
(C, [1, 1, 1, 1])
(B, [1, 1, 1, 1])
(D, [1])
(G, [1])

This is fed to the reducer to give the following output –

(A, 2)
(C, 4)
(B, 4)
(D, 1)
(G, 1)

The combiner can reduce the processing task or perform block-level reduction at the mapper only. If you consider the example given above, the combiner output for the case would be as follows –

Combiner 1 Output –

(B, 2)
(D, 1)
(C, 2)
(A, 1)

Combiner 2 Output –

(A, 1)
(C, 2)
(G, 1)
(B, 2)

The output of the combiner goes into the shuffling process to yield –

(A, [1, 1])
(C, [2, 2])
(B, [2, 2])
(D, [1])
(G, [1])

This is inputted to the reducer to give the following output –

(A, 2)
(C, 4)
(B, 4)

(D, 1)
(G, 1)

As is evident from the discussion, the reducer adds all the entries for characters at the block level. The combiner approach reduces the processing overhead of the reducer by performing a part of the computation at its level.

It is important to note that the combiner approach can be applied only to applications that allow the task breakdown at the data level. For instance, summation can be done without impacting the final result. On the other hand, the final result would vary for the two approaches if this computation were mean or median. Therefore, the former approach being the standard approach represents the correct answer. In such cases, the combiner approach shall fail.

The use of the combiner approach is entirely optional. Also, several aspects need to be taken into account before using this concept can be considered. Firstly, the combiner approach should yield the exact and correct result. Secondly, the combiner approach reduces the reducer overhead and data transfer cost.

However, it is essential to note that it increases the mapper's overhead. Therefore, the developer needs to analyze and compare the performance improvement using one approach over the other. For instance, if repetitions are low in the block (as is the case for the given example), using a combiner will only increase the overhead of the mapper without any substantial output.

The flow of execution after the implementation of partitioner and combiner will be as follows –

- Mapper -> Combiner -> Partitioner -> Reducer
- From the code perspective, the following points are noteworthy.
- Mapper is implemented by the Map Class
- Combiner is implemented by the Reduce Class

- Partitioner is implemented by the MyPartitioner Class (custom partitioning is implemented in this class)
- Reducer is implemented by the Reduce Class

4.4 MAP AND REDUCE SIDE JOINS

MapReduce program execution is a two-phase process – Map Phase and Reduce Phase. You may perform a join operation during the map phase, referred to as Map Side Join. Moreover, you may also wait until the Reduce Phase starts to perform the Join, and this type of join operation is termed Reduce Side Join.

4.4.1 Map Side Join

The most profound advantage of performing a Map Side Join is improved performance. With that said, performing such a join operation has its limitations. One of the considered datasets must be a small dataset to make this operation useful.

Scenarios where map side join can be used, include cases where one large table needs to be joined with a smaller table. For example, joining all data with a lookup table to create a report for the customer so that the smaller table can be easily duplicated for performing the join operation. Since mappers are individual tasks, they may need to access the data of the other mappers to perform the join task. At this point, the concept of distributed cache comes in.

4.4.2 Reduce Side Join

The limitation of a Map Side Join can be overcome by choosing a Reduce Side Join. However, in this case, performance is correspondingly compromised. Therefore, this is a trade-off that you need to figure out at your level while taking a call on which Side Join you must implement for your use case.

4.4.3 Map Side Join vs. Reduce Side Join

There may be scenarios where you may not be dealing with two large datasets. In such a case, the concept of distributed cache comes into the picture and can be extremely useful. The smaller dataset is made available to all the machines via distributed cache. In other words, you duplicate the smaller dataset on all the cluster nodes.

Bringing the large dataset into the picture can help in doing a better visualization of the scenario. The large dataset is fragmented and stored on different nodes of the cluster. The mapper tasks on each of these nodes also require access to the smaller dataset for processing. Therefore, the smaller dataset is copied onto each of the nodes and kept in the form of a local copy. Using this concept, the join operation can be performed right after the Map phase as the mapper looks up into the local copy of the second dataset, and you no longer have to wait until the Reduce phase ends to get the final output.

The reason why Map Side joins are performance-effective comes from the fact that the number of mappers is usually higher than the number of reducers. Therefore, performing a map side join allows much higher parallelism than its counterpart. However, such duplication is only feasible with small datasets, and thus, Map Side Joins are performed only if one of the datasets is small.

4.5 COUNTERS

Counters in MapReduce are lightweight objects typically used to keep track of the progress of executing map and reduce tasks. Moreover, they can also be used to track the data being processed, for example, the number of records successfully processed or the number of invalid records found. In totality, counters can be used for getting operational-level insights.

4.6 INPUT FORMATS

Typically, when an input is given to Hadoop, it is split, and the record reader reads the records to determine how they need to be stored. However, from the developer's point of view, the input splitting and record reading processes are taken care of by the framework based on the input format that the developer specifies. Once the framework performs these two processes, it feeds the input to the mapper. The class hierarchy of input formats is as follows –

1. File Input Format <K, V>
    a. Combine File Input Format <K, V>
       This format is usually used in scenarios where a number of small files have to be combined together to form splits.
    b. Text Input Format
       In this case, text files are given as input and the same are interpreted by the system as key-value pairs. This is the default input format as well.
    c. Key Value Text Input Format
       The input is available in the form of key value pairs separated by a delimiter.
    d. Nline Input Format
       If you wish to pass only a fixed number of lines as input to the mapper, then the Nline input format can be used. In this case, N is the number of lines that the mapper is instructed to take as input. It is generally used when input contains headers.
2. Sequence File Input Format <K, V>
   This format is a type of binary key-value format and can be given in the form of binary data, text data or input filter. Following are the sub-types of this input format –
    a. Sequence File as Binary Input Format
    b. Sequence File as Text Input Format
    c. Sequence File Input Filter <K, V>
3. Composite Input Format <K, V>
4. DB Input Format <T>
   The input is taken from a database.

Similarly, the output is generated after it is processed by the reducer, given to the RecordWriter and written to an output file. All these steps of the framework are determined by the output file format specified by the developer. The class hierarchy of output file formats is given below.

1. File Output Format <K, V>
   a. Text Output Format <K, V>
      The output is stored onto a text file.
   b. Sequence File Output Format <K, V>
      The output is stored onto a sequence file.
2. Null Output Format <K, V>
   If you don't want any output, then you can specify the output type, as Null Output and no output will be generated.
3. DB Output Format <K, V>
   Using this type, the output will be written onto a database.
4. Lazy Output Format <K, V>
   This file format allows the developer to instruct the framework to not create any zero-byte files as output. Therefore, it will not create a file until there is an output that has to be written onto the output file.

4.7 MRUNIT TESTING FRAMEWORK

Because the execution of MapReduce code involves many operational mappers, it is challenging to debug a faulty code. The MRUnit testing framework was developed by Cloudera and is a debugging tool that developers can use for this purpose. This testing framework provides four drivers for testing MapReduce code. These drivers include –

- MapDriver
- ReduceDriver
- MapReduceDriver
- PipelineMapReduceDriver

Most MapReduce developers have a Java programming background and are familiar with JUnit, a simple testing framework for Java. It is typically used for writing repeatable tests. This framework shares some commonalities with JUnit. Moreover, JUnit can be integrated to control log messages generated by the system better.

OBJECTIVE-TYPE QUESTIONS

1. Which of the following is implemented to reduce the traffic between the Mapper and Reducer?
   a. Partitioner
   b. Writable
   c. Combiner
   d. WritableComparable
2. Which of the following is/are driver(s) of MRUnit Testing Framework?
   a. MapDriver
   b. ReduceDriver
   c. MapReduceDriver
   d. All of the Above

SHORT ANSWER QUESTIONS

1. What is the difference between a split and block? Illustrate with the help of an example.
2. List the pros and cons of Map Side and Reduce Side Joins?
3. List a few use cases where counters can be implemented?
4. What is the default partitioning scheme? Explain with the help of an example.

LONG ANSWER QUESTIONS

1. Explain the difference between combiner and partitioner? Also illustrate diagrammatically, with the help of an example, the flow of execution when partitioner and combiner are implemented?

Chapter 5

PIG

OBJECTIVES

- Introduction to Pig
- Key Characteristics of Pig
- Limitations of Pig
- Common Use-cases
- Pig Commands and Scripting

5.1 INTRODUCTION TO PIG

Pig is an open-source, high-level data-flow system. It is an abstraction tool that allows users to perform complicated MapReduce tasks without the need to write elaborate MapReduce programs. *Pig Latin* is a data manipulation language used to query and manipulate data within the Pig Shell. Companies like Yahoo, Microsoft, and Google extensively use this tool.

5.2 THE YAHOO! STORY

Yahoo was one of the first companies to adopt Hadoop for solving their big data problem. However, they realized that any task that needs to be performed in Hadoop must be coded in MapReduce. However, data scientists at Yahoo did not know how to code in MapReduce. Therefore, they had to contact MapReduce developers for coding every task. In order to reduce this dependency, Yahoo developed an abstraction tool that works over Hadoop called Pig.

5.3 KEY CHARACTERISTICS

Key characteristics of Pig include –

1. Open-source
2. Simple
   Java is not simple to program and requires high level of programming expertise to code. Pig abstracts Java code, reducing programming effort substantially on part of the developer. It is a convenient ad-hoc way for creating and executing MapReduce jobs on large datasets.
3. Hassle-free development
   The syntax and programming style of Pig is similar to that of SQL, which is a popular processing language used by data scientists. Moreover, several built-in operators like JOIN, GROUP and SORT are available in Pig, which can be used. This allows easier and faster development.
4. Can process all kinds of data
   Pig is capable of handling structured, semi-structured and unstructured data. This is perhaps the reason why this tool is named Pig. Just like the Pig can eat anything, this tool can take in any kind of data. However, there is an exception to this statement. This tool cannot process audio and video data.
5. Extensible
   The power of Pig is unlimited in view of the fact that apart from the predefined functions available in Pig, it also supports User Defined Functions (UDFs), which can be written in Java, Python, JavaScript and Ruby.

5.4 PERFORMANCE: PIG VS. MAPREDUCE

Pig is a generic framework for data processing. Therefore, the underlying code for performing MapReduce tasks is designed and developed to support a range of applications. On the other hand, when you code in MapReduce, you design and develop the code according to your use-case.

Therefore, the MapReduce code specially designed for your application is obviously more performance-optimized than a corresponding Pig script. With that said, if the application requires standard MapReduce task execution, then Pig will perform just as well as its MapReduce counterpart. It is important to mention here that the starting overhead for Pig has been neglected for this comparison.

5.5 LIMITATIONS

Like any other tool, Pig also has its share of limitations, which include –

- It cannot process completely unstructured data like audio and video.
- It should not be used for applications where performance is an issue.
- It should not be used for applications where you need control over the base implementation and the way it is being done.

5.6 APPLICATIONS

Typical applications of Pig include –

- Performing adhoc queries on large datasets
- Data processing for large search engines
- Processing of web-logs
- Quick prototyping of algorithms for processing large datasets

5.7 WORKING WITH PIG

Pig is an interface that picks up data from HDFS, executes it in the form of MapReduce jobs on the cluster and returns results to the user. Therefore, Pig resides on the system and executes jobs on the Hadoop cluster. The dataflow diagram for Pig operation is illustrated in Fig. 5.1.

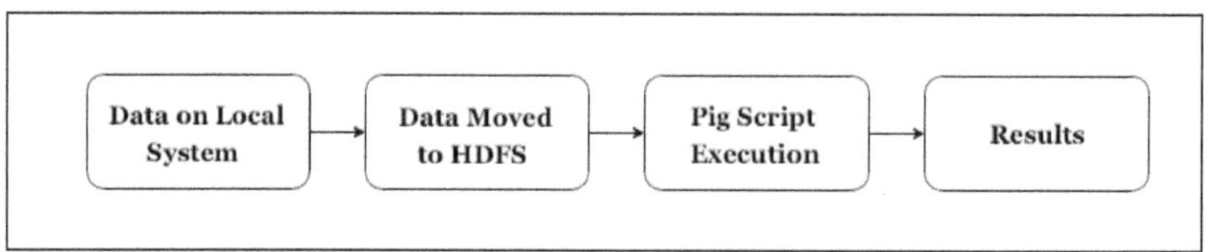

Fig. 5.1 Pig Dataflow Diagram

Since, Pig picks up data for processing from HDFS, data needs to be first transferred from the local filesystem to HDFS. It is on this data that Pig script runs and provides the desired results to the user. A Pig script is a list of Pig commands that are executed one after another. Pig commands can also be individually run inside the Pig Shell, which is an interactive interface between the user and execution engine. It is important to understand that Pig abstracts MapReduce code for easier coding, but it is not possible to see the actual MapReduce code that is run for a specific Pig task. The basic Pig program structure is shown in Fig. 5.2.

Pig has two components, which are as follows –

- Pig Compiler
  Dataflow is expressed in Pig using Pig Latin. The commands are compiled using the Pig compiler.
- Execution Environment
  The commands, which are basically MapReduce tasks can be executed in one of the following modes –
  - Distributed mode
    In this mode, MapReduce jobs are executed on the Hadoop cluster.

- Local mode

  In this mode, MapReduce jobs are executed on the JVM of the local machine.

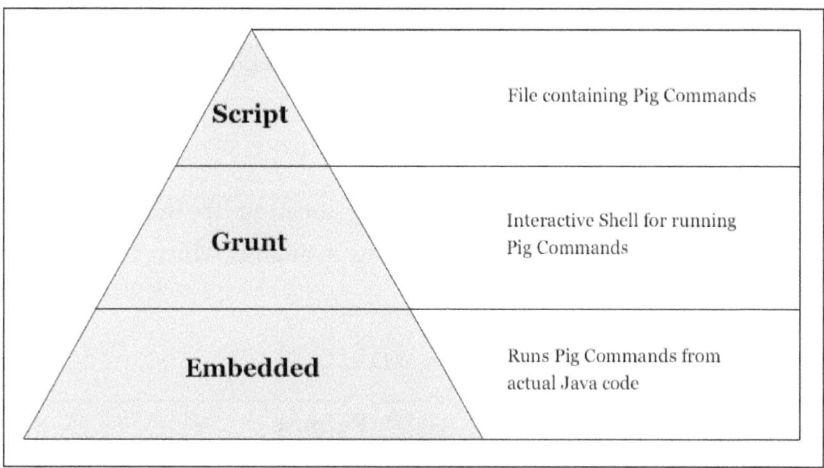

Fig. 5.2 Pig Program Structure

5.7.1 Data Models

Apart from the basic datatypes like int, float and char, three other complex datatypes also exist in Pig. These datatypes include Bag, Tuple and Map. In order to help you understand these data models and their relevance to the diverse applications that Pig supports, let us take a brief look at the four basic data models, mentioned in Table 5.1.

Table. 5.1 Basic Data Models

Data Model	Description
Data Map	Key-value pairs
Field	Piece of data
Tuple	Ordered set of fields
Bag	Collection of tuples

Let us take the following example of a data set –

T = (1, {(2, 3), (4, 6), (5, 7)}, ['apache': 'search'])

<-FIELD-> < -TUPLE->

<-------------------BAG---------------------> <--DATA MAP-->

5.7.2 File Loaders

Data needs to be loaded from the base location to the Pig Shell for processing. For this, several data loaders are available, which are mentioned in Table 5.2.

Table. 5.2 List of Data Loaders

File Loader	Purpose
BinStorage	Binary storage
PigStorage	Loads and stores data with a specified delimiter
TextLoader	Loads data line by line (newline is the delimiter)
CSVLoader	Loads CSV
XMLLoader	Loads XML

5.7.3 Commonly Used Operators

Some operators along with their functions are specified in Table 5.3 for your reference.

Table. 5.3 Pig Operators

Operator Type	Operators
Arithmetic Operators	+, *, -, /, ?:, %
Cast Operators	Transfomation of one data type to another
Boolean Operators	and, not, or
Comparison Operators	!=, ==, <, >, <=, >=, matches

Operator Type	Operators
Dereference Operators	dereference bags (bag.id or bag.(id,...)), tuples (tuple.id or tuple.(id,...)) and maps (map#'key')
Construction Operators	Used for creating map [], bag {} and tuple ()
Flatten Operator	Flatten un-nests tuples as well as bags
Disambiguate Operator	(::) used to identification of field names after COGROUP, JOIN, FLATTEN or CROSS operators
Sign Operators	– -> changes the sign of a number
Null Operator	is null, is not null
LOAD	Loads data from the file system
JOIN	Performs an inner join of two or more relations based on common field values
IMPORT	Import macros defined in a separate file
FOREACH	Generates transformation of data for each row as specified
FILTER	Selects tuples from a relation based on some condition
DISTINCT	Removes duplicate tuples in a relation
CROSS	Computes the cross product of two or more relations
COGROUP/GROUP	Groups the data in one or more relations
STREAM	Sends data to an external script or program
STORE	Stores or saves results to the file system
SPLIT	Partitions a relation into two or more relations based on some expression
SAMPLE	Partitions a relation into two or more relations, selects a random data
ORDERBY	Sorts a relation based on one or more fields
MAPREDUCE	Executes native MapReduce jobs inside a Pig script
UNION	Computes the union of two or more relations

5.7.4 Diagnostic Operators and UDF

Operators and UDF Statements along with their functions are specified in Table 5.4 for your reference.

Table. 5.4 Diagnostic Operators and UDF Statements

Operator	Purpose
describe	Gives schema details
explain	Gives logical/physical plan and how the job is going to run
illustrate	Gives step by step illustration of how the data is being changed from its original form
register	Registers jar file with Pig
define	Creates alias for UDF

5.7.5 Functions

Pig provides many functions to perform varied tasks. Commonly used functions have been described in Table 5.5. Besides these, there are functions for LOAD/STORE, MATH, STRING and BAG/TUPLE/MAP operations.

Table. 5.5 Commonly Used Functions

Function	Use
AVG(expression)	Calculates averages of values in a single column bag
COUNT(expression)	Calculates the number of elements in a bag (null values are ignored)
CONCAT(expression, expression)	Concatenates expressions that are identical in type
DIFF(expression, expression)	Compares two fields in a tuple and returns all the fields that are not identical
IsEmpty(expression)	Checks if a map or bag is empty
MAX(expression)	Determines the maximum numeric value in a single column bag
MIN(expression)	Determines the minimum numeric value in a single column bag

Function	Use
SIZE(expression)	Determines the number of elements in a data type and includes null values
TOKENIZE(expression [,'field_delimiter'])	Splits an expression on the basis of the specified delimiter
SUM(expression)	Calculates sum of values in a single column bag

5.7.6 User Defined Functions (UDF)

In order to provide extensibility to the architecture, Pig allows users to contribute functions to the base framework using UDFs or User Defined functions. The open source nature of Pig attracts contributions from many users and developers and all these UDFs are added to PiggyBank.jar. The operators specifically used for UDF creation are described in the Table 5.6.

Table. 5.6 UDF Operators

Operator	Purpose
Register	Registers jar file with Pig
Define	Creates alias for UDF

OBJECTIVE-TYPE QUESTIONS

1. Which company developed Pig?

    a. Google
    b. Microsoft
    c. Yahoo
    d. None of the above

2. Pig Latin is similar to which of the following languages?

    a. Java
    b. Python
    c. JavaScript
    d. SQL

3. Which of the following types of data cannot be processed using Pig?
    a. Audio
    b. Video
    c. Both a and b
    d. None of the above
4. Pig supports which of the following data models?
    a. Bag
    b. Tuple
    c. Map
    d. All of the above

SHORT ANSWER QUESTIONS

1. Which types of data can be analyzed using Pig?
2. Can Pig be considered a replacement for MapReduce?
3. Pig can operate in two modes. Name the two modes of operation and explain the difference?

LONG ANSWER QUESTIONS

1. Describe the key characteristics of Pig and explain how the architecture is extensible?
2. Is the performance of Pig comparable with MapReduce under all scenarios? If no, give example of scenarios where Pig can perform better, comparable and worse than MapReduce?
3. Does Pig reside on the local machine or the Hadoop cluster? How are Pig Scripts executed in the execution environment?

Chapter 6

HIVE

OBJECTIVES

- Basics of Hive
- Differences between Hive and Pig
- Differences between Hive and Traditional RDBMS
- Hive Architecture
- Introduction to Hive Scripting

6.1 BACKGROUND

Hive is a MapReduce abstraction tool developed by Facebook, similar to Pig. Although the objective of these two tools is the same, they follow different approaches. Data scientists who have some experience in programming prefer Pig. On the other hand, while Hive is for data scientists who have experience of working in SQL. Hive scripting is done using HiveQL. These scripts are read by the Hive driver and are converted into MapReduce jobs, which are eventually executed on the Hadoop cluster.

6.2 THE FACEBOOK STORY

Before switching to Hadoop, Facebook used Oracle DB and SQL Server for its database management needs. Data were collected from Oracle DB, and ETL (Extraction, Transformation, and Loading) was performed using a hard-coded python script. The complex coding of the solution made it impossible for the system to scale to the increasing data storage and management requirements. Moreover, Facebook generates a wide variety and velocity data, which is also an essential requirement for any tool developed.

6.2.1 Challenges Faced by Facebook

Apart from the scaling problem faced by Facebook, a few other challenges had to be resolved to get a complete solution to the problem at hand. These challenges include –

- The number of users is large.
- Data is generated in huge volumes daily.
- Huge numbers of queries are made to Facebook daily.
- The data generated by Facebook also includes vast volumes of multimedia data (audio and video).

In order to solve this problem, Facebook came up with two probable solutions. Firstly, Facebook had the option to continue with an RDBMS solution. However, this solution was inadequate when meeting the storage and processing needs of this rapidly evolving data system. The other option available was to migrate to Hadoop. However, as are the challenges faced during any technological migration, Facebook did not have trained staff for Hadoop. Moreover, coding in Hadoop was also not an easy task, and the ramp-up of its employees from their existing SQL expertise to Hadoop was expected to be a slow and time-consuming process.

6.2.2 Hive for Facebook

Migration from RDBMS to Hadoop could have been more straightforward by creating a tool that can be programmed like SQL and works on top of the Hadoop ecosystem, thereby achieving the required performance without needing an extensive upgrade of technical knowledge. It is for this reason that Hive was created. It is noteworthy that Facebook uses Hive only for structured data analysis. Other MapReduce APIs deal with image, audio, and multimedia data.

6.3 HIVE BASICS

Hive is a data-warehousing package that works over and above Hadoop. It would not be wrong to state that Hive is an abstraction tool that requires no prior knowledge of Hadoop or Java to program. This tool is typically used for data analysis, and target users include data scientists who have experience of working in SQL. This feature is attributed to the fact that HiveQL, the query language used for Hive, is similar to SQL. Hive is extremely useful for managing and querying structured data. Please note that Hive does not support update and selective delete operations.

Key features of Hive are illustrated in Fig. 6.1. Other key features of Hive include –

- Schema flexibility is easy to achieve.
- It provides partitioning and bucketing features to allow convenient handling of large volumes of data.
- The inbuilt capabilities available in Hive can be easily improved.
- JDBC/ODBC drivers allow querying of dataflow from any platform outside Hadoop. Therefore, Hive improves data accessibility.
- Hive tables are created in HDFS. Therefore, there is no need to move data, making it an appropriate solution for large-scale data analysis.

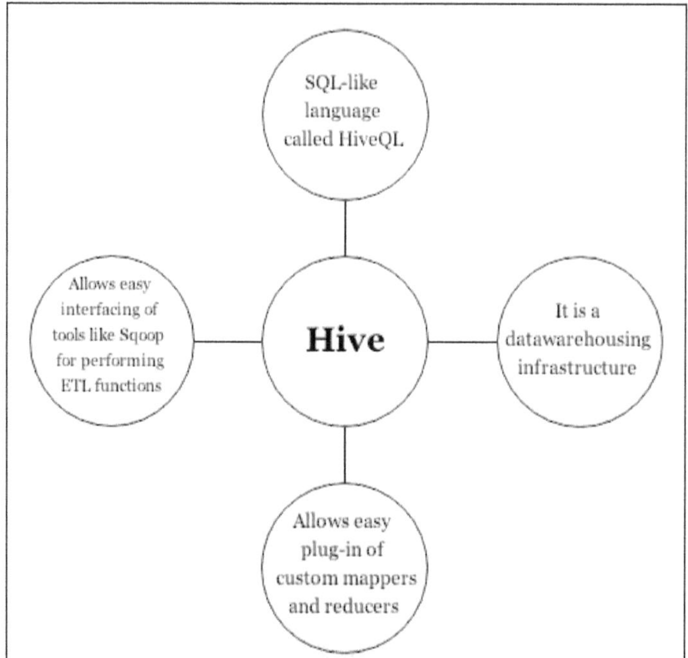

Fig. 6.1 Key Features of Hive

Some common applications of Hive include –

- Log processing
- Document indexing
- Data mining
- Predictive modeling
- Business intelligence applications

6.4 DIFFERENCES BETWEEN HIVE AND PIG

Fundamental differences exist between Pig and Hive. These include –

- Hive requires explicit definition of schemas before they are used. However, in the absence of an explicit schema definition, implicit definitions are taken. On the other hand, Pig allows users to define schemas.
- Hive works in HDFS alone while Pig can be run in local or HDFS mode.

HiveQL and Pig Latin differ in the following ways –

- Pig Latin follows the procedural approach. In other words, the developer for execution lays out a step-by-step procedure. For example, data processing is a three-step process: (1) data is loaded (2) data is analyzed (3) result is generated. Commands for each of these steps are given in the order specified while programming in Pig Latin. On the other hand, HiveQL is declarative.
- Pig Latin is a language preferred by developers who have programming experience while HiveQL is the language of choice for data scientists with little or no programming experience.

Some of the features that Hive possesses, but Pig lacks include –

- Web Interface
- JDBC/ODBC Drivers
- Partitions
- Server (Server is optional in Hive, but it doesn't exist in Pig)

6.5 DIFFERENCES BETWEEN HIVE AND TRADITIONAL RDBMS

In Hive, schema is verified when a query is made, unlike in RDBMS where the schema is verified when the data is loaded. As a result, the initial load is faster in Hive as compared to traditional RDBMS. Moreover, it also supports indexes and updates, which are not available otherwise.

6.6 HIVE ARCHITECTURE

Hive architecture describes the different layers of Hadoop and its support for Hive. As mentioned previously, Hive works on top of Hadoop. Therefore, the base layer is Hadoop. Precisely, Hive operates solely on HDFS. For every table created in Hive, the schema for the table along with other table parameters is stored in the form of metadata.

The Metastore component of Hive architecture maintains metadata for all the tables in Hive. It is important to mention that the actual data is stored in HDFS only. Any SQL technology like MySQL may be used for

Metastore. Besides Metastore, another component on the same layer is Driver, which takes SQL scripting and compiles, optimizes and executes it for the user. All of these operations will be performed against the metadata stored in the Metastore to get access to actual data in HDFS.

On top of this layer, the next layer has a thrift server, which allows communication from the outside world. It allows JDBC/ODBC drivers to operate and enables querying of the system from outside via Karmasphere, Hue, and other similar technologies. Fig. 6.2 illustrates Hive Architecture.

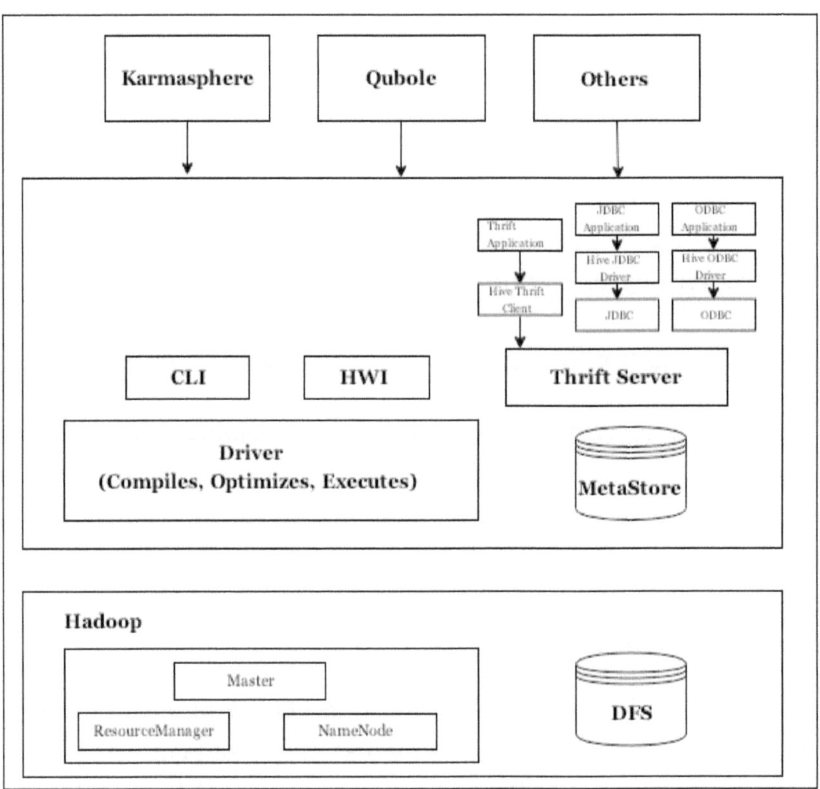

Fig. 6.2 Hive Architecture

6.7 COMPONENTS OF HIVE

Basically, Hive has five components namely, Shell, Driver, Metastore, Compiler and Execution Engine (shown in Fig. 6.3). Driver and

Metastore have been described previously. The other components include Shell, Compiler and Execution Engine. The compiler compiles the SQL statements while the Execution engine executes the queries. On the other hand, shell provides an interface to the user for inputting queries.

Fig. 6.3 Hive Components

Metastore can be deployed in many different ways. The default deployment is the derby database. Besides this, MySQL, in local or remote mode, may also be used for maintaining metadata.

6.8 LIMITATIONS OF HIVE

Hive suffers from limitations and it is important for developers to be aware of these to make optimal use of this tool. These limitations include –

- It cannot be used for online transaction processing.
- It does not support real-time queries.
- It does not allow row-level updates.
- High latency (of the order of minutes)

6.9 HIVE SCRIPTING

The Hive Query Language allows users to perform basic SQL-like operations. Some of the common functions possible with HiveQL include –

- Filter rows using WHERE clause
- Equijoin two tables
- Store the results from a query into another table
- Store the results from a query in HDFS directory
- Table and partitions can be managed using operations like CREATE, DROP and ALTER

Although, the time taken to give results is higher with Hive, the capabilities of this tool outweigh those of its counterparts.

6.9.1 Basic Datatypes

Hive supports many primitive and complex datatypes. The primitive datatypes supported include Boolean, Integer, Float and String. Moreover, complex datatypes like Structs, Arrays and Maps are also supported. An important point to mention here is that Hive does not require normalized data for basic operations.

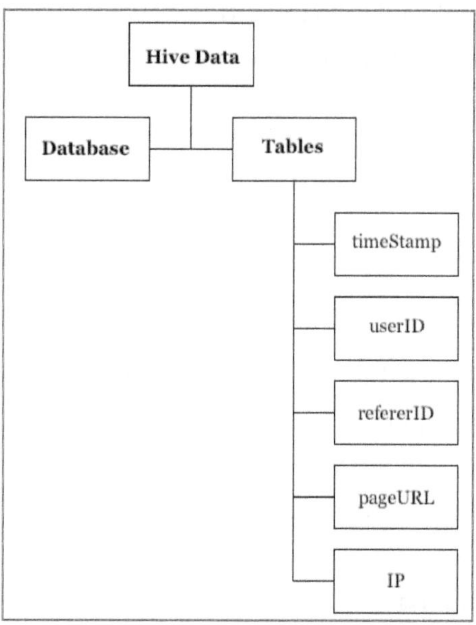

Fig. 6.4 Hive Table Parameters

6.9.2 Data Models

Data in Hive is stored in the form of tables inside databases. Therefore, databases are namespaces and tables are schemas under namespaces. Fig. 6.4 shows the parameters that are saved for each table in Hive.

6.9.3 Partitioning and Bucketing

Hive provides two special features namely partitions and buckets. Partitioning allows grouping of databases on the basis of some column(s). It is just a technique that defines how data is stored in HDFS. Partitions can further be divided on the basis of columns to form buckets. This technique is used for data sampling. The objective of using both these techniques is to reduce the response time for query processing.

While processing large datasets, Hive needs to process queries on them. For example, there may be the need to run the query, *SELECT * FROM table1 WHERE geo = 'USA'*, on four files namely file1.txt, file2.txt, file3.txt and file4.txt. In order to execute this query, Hive scans through all the records of these four files. The performance of such an operation can be optimized if the data is already partitioned on the basis of geographical location (column: geo). Partitions inside the directories may look like:

user/hive/warehouse/<DB_NAME>/<TABLE_NAME>/geo=USA/<only USA data>

user/hive/warehouse/<DB_NAME>/<TABLE_NAME>/geo=USA/<only UK data>

user/hive/warehouse/<DB_NAME>/<TABLE_NAME>/geo=USA/<only INDIA data>

In other words, if we know how the users will eventually query the data, we can partition data in such a manner that optimal performance can be achieved for the system. To determine the most appropriate partitioning scheme for a system, most frequent queries made by users need to be scanned. Hive also supports multi-level partitioning. Partitions inside the directories for multi-level partitioning may look like:

user/hive/warehouse/<DB_NAME>/<TABLE_NAME>/geo=USA/ state=CA/<only CA, USA data>

user/hive/warehouse/<DB_NAME>/<TABLE_NAME>/geo=USA/ state=ARZ<only ARZ, USA data>

A partition key defines each partition. Moreover, it is conventional to use date for naming partitions. This makes it easy for the developer to identify and distinguish between partitions. Internally, every time a partition is created, Hive rearranges data and creates corresponding folders and files for the partition. For example, when a partition is made for each unique value of column:geo, a slice of data is created corresponding to each partition in the system.

As mentioned previously, the partitioning scheme is determined by the requirements of the application or as specified by the user. However, there may arise a scenario where the user states that he or she is most likely to query on column:ID, which possesses unique value for every record stored in the system. Partitioning done for this column will create a partition for every record on the system. This will result in creation of endless files and folders, leading to unaccounted overhead.

To handle such cases, the concept of bucketing was introduced. In scenarios where partitioning is desired on column with unique values, high level buckets are created and groups of records that fall under these buckets are assigned to them. The process of bucketing is performed in the following manner.

1. Determine the number of buckets that need to be created.
2. Calculate the hash value for each unique value of the selected column using the following formula:
   Hash_Value = Column_Val % (Bucket_Size)
3. Depending on the hash value, a bucket is assigned to the record.

4. When a query is made, the hash value is again calculated for the column value to determine the bucket in which the record is placed. The records in that bucket are searched for the desired record.

In order to understand the concept better, let us take an example. Say 5 buckets need to be created and bucketing is done for column:ID. Therefore, the bucketing process will result in the creation of buckets: 0, 1, 2, 3 and 4. Hash value for ID1 is calculated by applying modulo function using the following formula:

Hash_Value = ID1 % 5

Similarly hash values are calculated for all records and corresponding buckets are assigned to them. Please note that partitioning and bucketing can be performed together. Moreover, none of these strategies make changes to data. They simply rearrange data for faster querying.

OBJECTIVE-TYPE QUESTIONS

1. What is Hive?

   a. Data Loading Tool
   b. Abstraction Tool for MapReduce
   c. Data Processing Tool
   d. Both b and c

2. Which component of Hive allows querying of Hive data from other platforms like Qubole and Karmasphere?

   a. JDBC/ODBC Drivers
   b. Thrift Server
   c. Driver
   d. None of the above

3. Which two features of Hive give developers the control to optimize system performance by analyzing most frequent queries?
   a. Partitioning
   b. Bucketing
   c. Both a and b
   d. Neither a nor b
4. Which is by default used for metadata management in Hive?
   a. MySQL (Locally)
   b. MySQL (Remotely)
   c. Derby Database
   d. None of the above

SHORT ANSWER QUESTIONS

1. Both Pig and Hive are abstraction tools, serving almost the same purpose. What was the need for Hive when Pig could solve the problem?
2. Does Hive have any limitations? If yes, please elaborate?
3. Facebook uses Hive only for data analysis of structured data. Is it because Hive is not capable of handling unstructured or semi-structured data?

LONG ANSWER QUESTIONS

1. Explain how Hive differs from Pig and traditional RDBMSs in capability?
2. Explain the architecture of Hive, giving brief insights on the function of each of the components?
3. What is the need of partitioning? Also, explain how bucketing caters for a special scenario of partitioning?

Chapter 7

NOSQL DATABASES AND HBASE

OBJECTIVES

- Need for HBase and NoSQL Databases
- Types of NoSQL Databases
- Basics of HBase
- HBase Storage Architecture
- Need for Zookeeper
- Working in HBase

7.1 INTRODUCTION

Change in data processing requirements and data types initiated research in the field of databases other than SQL. It is not possible to fit every data into the table-column format. This made research in the field of NoSQL databases relevant. Hadoop also required a database that could run over its framework, which gave rise to HBase. It is important to note that NoSQL databases are not just limited to HBase for Hadoop. There are a range of NoSQL database solutions, which include MongoDB and Cassandra, among others.

Companies like Facebook and Yahoo faced challenges with respect to storage and processing of increasing volumes of data with traditional database management systems. With traditional systems, the performance of the system is good when it is first installed. However, the performance of the system deteriorates as the amount of data that it has to deal with increases.

In order to improve the system performance, lateral approaches like addition of a caching layer and reduction of RDBMS constraints, by getting rid of index, are done. Besides this, joins can be avoided by using de-normalized tables. The performance can still be improved if you read only pre-computed table data and do not perform any particular operation on the table. However, restricting the functionality to this level for meeting minimum performance levels makes the whole point of using RDBMS meaningless. The key benefits of RDBMS are lost along the way.

When Google was indexing all the data to enable searching at mammoth-like magnitude and improve the scalability of the system, the journey of HBase started. To start with, Google gave the concept of BigTable in the form of a whitepaper, which later graduated to become Apache HBase.

7.2 NEED FOR HBASE

The requirement of such databases arises from the emergence of platforms like Twitter and Facebook, which require handling of large databases along with features where users can update, add and delete data. The use of Hadoop allows big data management, but it restricts the user from interacting with its ecosystem in real-time. Moreover, selective updates and deletes cannot be made in Hadoop.

HBase addresses the limitations of Hadoop providing support for large volume of data, offering high fault tolerance and providing high scalability, reliability and flexibility. Besides this, it has an in-memory component (MemStore). Therefore, real-time data access is possible, which allows operations like create, update and delete. We had mentioned previously that Hadoop does not support selective update and delete. However, with HBase, all these operations have become possible.

Many real-world applications like giving recommendations to users on retail web-portals and ad targeting require handling of huge datasets in fraction of seconds. For example, if we talk about ad targeting, then a user views a product on one of the Ecommerce websites like eBay. Now, the ad follows the user on any website that he or she opens unless he or she views it again or acts on it. In order to implement this kind of functionality, many dataset interactions need to take place in less than a second to generate the desired results within allowable time limits.

With conventional RDBMS, many tables need to be maintained corresponding to each user and when processing needs to be performed for a particular user, many table interactions need to be made. On the other hand, Hadoop manages a single table for all users and connections between users in the same table need to be exploited to implement such functionality. While a traditional RDBMS will take a long time to generate result, Hadoop will do the required even before the user realizes that the result has been specially generated for him or her.

It is important to understand that most applications like recommendation generation, ad targeting and fault detection, among others, have a common set of requirements, which include –

1. Handling of large datasets
2. Data needs to be accessed on random basis. For example, you may want to access your Facebook post from last year or the year before that or any post you want to access for that matter. This type of access is called random access.
3. Handling of different types of data (structured, semi-structured and unstructured data)
4. Ability to handle variable schema
   Social media portals like Facebook and Twitter have immensely evolved over time. They have improved their features, added many new features and removed things that have proven to become obsolete. However, in the process, the schema of the tables that they use to store their data has also changed. With that said, they

could not do away with all the existing data because users wanted their old data intact. In order to update schema in traditional RDBMS systems, new tables with the updated schema need to be created before data can be transferred from the old table to the new table. This is a tedious and complicated task. On the other hand, HBase allows variable schema for different rows with the table as well, making it extremely simple to work with changing schema requirements of the system.

5. Data compression
   Understandably, when we are working with huge datasets, automatic data compression must be performed.
6. Support for automatic distribution of data
   When we are dealing with big data insertions, it is not possible to insert all the data first and then distribute it for further use. This shall fail the whole purpose of data distribution. Therefore, the system must perform automatic data distribution upon insertion.

If we had to use traditional RDBMS systems to fulfill these requirements, then we will have to make individual tables for each user that includes data about the user and a table that maintains the activity of the user during a session or whenever a connection was established. On the other hand, HBase stores all the information for a user in the same row of the table. Therefore, all you need to do is access this row. A better solution must have the following –

- Distributed database
- Automatic data distribution
- Automatic data sorting
  In order to help you understand this, let us have a look at the data that we will probably be storing for a user connection/session. Evidently, this data will have timestamp values attached to them. The database must automatically sort the data in such a manner that recent entries are on top. This will make data retrieval faster as most processing shall take place on recent sessions' data.

- Handling for sparse data source
  This requirement is in view of the fact that support for variable schema results in data variations of the order that one row might have only a few entries while another row might have hundreds of entries. Therefore, for the former row, the rest of the entries are NULL and the database must be able to handle this on its own.

HBase provides an apt solution in view of these requirements as –

- It is based on Hadoop. Therefore, distributed database and automatic distribution of data comes naturally to it.
- HBase uses sparse matrix to store data. Therefore, for any data that is NULL, nothing is stored, but on need basis, it can go back and re-compute to find if data for that entry was NULL.
- Sorted storage of data is supported in HBase.

7.3 CLASSIFICATION OF NOSQL DATABASES

The common thing between all NoSQL databases is that they don't support SQL. The four categories of NoSQL databases are given below.

7.3.1 Key-Value Stores

In such databases, all the operations are performed using a key. For example, if you have a session database, then data retrieval from this table will be via SessionID, the key for the table.

- Databases:
  Dynamo (Amazon)
- Dynamo is Amazon's offering. They provide it in the form of Database-as-a-Service.
- MemBase
- CitrusLeaf
- Voldemort (LinkedIn)
- Riak

7.3.2 Big Data Clones

This class of NoSQL databases is completely based on the Google's whitepaper that introduced BigTable concept. Databases that fall under this category include –

- HBase
  It is an Apache project that is implemented in Java. We will discuss this database in detail later in the chapter.
- BigTable (Google)
  This is the base project, which is based on the whitepaper published by Google.
- Hypertable
  It is a C++ implementation of the Google's whitepaper.
- Cassandra
  Facebook developed this database system. The team that developed Cassandra was also a part of the development team of Amazon's DynamoDB. Therefore, Cassandra is majorly a combination of BigTable and DynamoDB.

7.3.3 Document Databases

This class of databases is extremely useful for storing data in XML or JSON format and it includes the following –

- MongoDB
- CouchOne
- OrientDB
- TerraStore

7.3.4 Graph Databases

These databases are based on the graph concept. The best use-case for such databases is social media network that can be simulated in the form of a graph with users as vertices and connections between them as edges. The graph concept is an efficient method for managing social media data. Included solutions are –

- FlockDB
- Neo4J
- InfoGrid
- Sones

7.3.5 CAP Theorem

The decision of which database to use from the given list is majorly dependent on your performance and system requirements. CAP theorem is a standard approach that is used for assistance in making such decisions. The CAP theorem uses three parameters namely, consistency, availability and partition tolerance and states that it is possible to get only two of these characteristics in a NoSQL solution. Therefore, the decision of which database to use must be purely based on which characteristics are important for you. The three characteristics are as follows –

1. Consistency
   The commits performed in a database are atomic across the whole database.
2. Availability
   The database is available and accessible at all times.
3. Partition Tolerance
   The system responds correctly in all conditions except when there is a total network failure.
4. The distribution of databases across these characteristics is illustrated in Fig. 7.1.

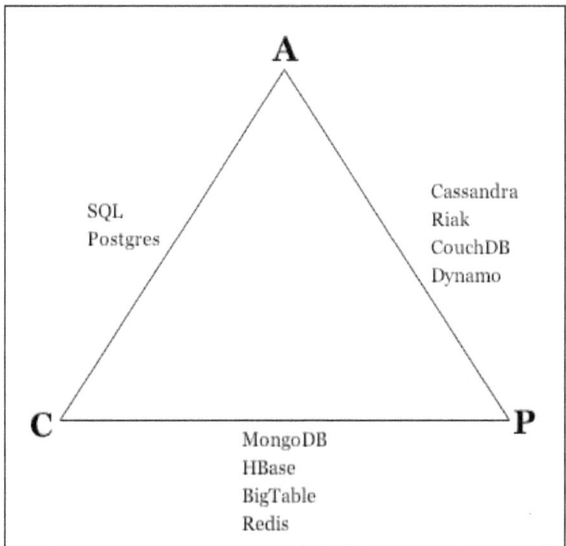

Fig. 7.1 Databases and CAP Characteristics

In HBase, the data is consistent and the database offers good partition tolerance, but if the master goes down, the data will no longer be available. This makes HBase an appropriate solution for applications where data availability can be compromised.

7.4 DEFINING HBASE

HBase is a NoSQL database (non-relational) in which key-value stores are used for storing data. Other main features of HBase include –

- Distributed Database
  The underlying uses of Hadoop's HDFS makes HBase a distributed database.
- Sparse
  The use of sparse matrices to store data allows HBase to manage NULL values without actually storing them. Thus, it is also referred to as a sparse database.
- Multi-dimensional
  Data is stored in HBase with the following dimensions: row, column, column family and timestamp. Moreover, multiple

versions of data can be stored with the help of timestamp dimension. An example of how storage of multiple versions of data is useful is the status message stored in Whatsapp or Google hangouts. You can set a status message, change it and still access the status messages you had previously set.

- Sorted Map
  The data stored in HBase is automatically sorted in such a manner that recent data appears first.
- Consistent
  HBase offers high consistency.

Since, HBase uses Hadoop's HDFS at the back-end. Hence, it is commonly referred to as Hadoop database. HBase stores the data in column family, therefore, the name, column-oriented database. Moreover, it uses the concept of key-value pairs and thus, it is also referred to as key-value store.

7.4.1 How HBase Came Into Existence

The HBase journey started in the year 2006, when Google published the BigTable whitepaper. Henceforth, it evolved as a sub-project of Hadoop. However, with Hadoop 2.x, HBase was converted into a full-fledged project, releasing HBase 0.92 in 2011.

7.4.2 Difference Between HBase and RDBMS

Key differences between HBase and traditional RDBMS systems include –

- HBase is column-oriented while RDBMSs are mostly row-oriented.
- HBase allows variable schema, which is not possible with RDBMS. Moreover, columns can be added on the fly with HBase.
- RDBMSs are not optimized for sparse tables and handling NULLs will impose immense overhead while HBase's use of sparse matrices for data storage equips it for handling of sparse tables.
- In order to perform join in HBase, MapReduce programming needs to be done. However, RDBMS is optimized for performing

joins. In view of this, HBase is tightly integrated with MapReduce, which is not the case for RDBMS.

- One of the most significant differences between these two databases is that HBase is horizontally scalable. With increasing data and complexity, more hardware can be employed to meet the changing performance needs of the system. This feature is totally absent in RDBMS.
- Lastly, RDBMSs are tailor-made for structured data, but HBase can handle structured as well as semi-structured data.

7.5 USES OF HBASE

Some of the main uses of HBase include –

- Offers high scalability
- Can store multiple versions of data
- Can be used for structured, semi-structured and unstructured data
- Can be used for storing extremely high volumes of data
- Data gets stored in a column-oriented manner, making column-based analysis easier to perform. Therefore, applications that require such an analysis can make use of HBase.
- Generate data from MapReduce workflow

Companies like Facebook, Twitter and Yahoo make use of HBase. For example, Yahoo uses HBase to detect document near-duplicates using document fingerprints. On the other hand, Facebook uses HBase to power their message infrastructure and Twitter internally generates data for applications like people search using HBase.

7.6 LIMITATIONS OF HBASE

HBase offers limited functionality in some scenarios. These include –

- HBase is not a performance-effective solution for small volumes of data
- It lacks RDBMS commands and there is no SQL support. Only API calls are supported.

- When the cluster is small, say of 5 nodes and replication factor is 3. In such a scenario, HBase is not a good solution.

7.7 COMPONENTS OF HBASE

HBase has the master-slave architecture. It has three main components (as shown in Fig. 7.2), which are as follows –

- HBaseMaster
  This component controls the whole process of where the data will be stored. Therefore, HBaseMaster manages the HBase cluster.
- HRegionServer
  The data is actually stored across multiple machines called the HBaseRegionServer.
- HBaseClient
  Users can interact with HBase through a Java program using API via HBaseClients.

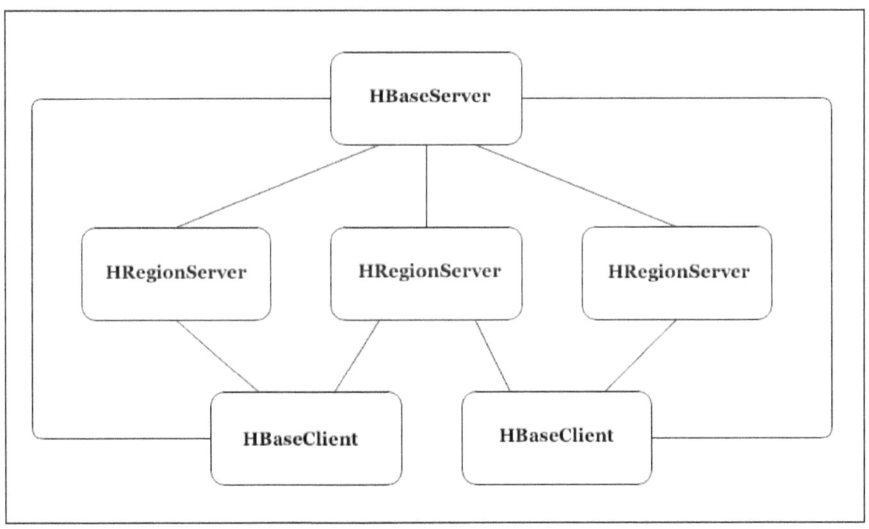

Fig. 7.2 Components of HBase

Data is distributed in HBase by dividing the same into regions. For example, if there is a table that needs to be stored in HBase and it has rows from A1 to Z50, then this data can be divided into three regions, which may or may not have same number of rows in it. For example, region-1: A1-A5, region-2: A6-F50, region-3: F51-Z50. All these regions will be stored on different HRegionServers. It is important to understand that HRegionServer can have one or more regions on it. HRegionServer uses Hadoop's HDFS and consists of two sub-components namely Write-Ahead Log (WAL) and HFiles. ZooKeeper does the management of storage and processing in HBase.

7.7.1 Writing Data Into HBase

Whenever a write operation is performed, it is done against MemStore, which is an in-memory write buffer, and Write-Ahead Log (WAL). Clients cannot interact with HFiles directly as far as writes are concerned. Therefore, whenever a write needs to be performed, data is given to MemStore and correspondingly the same data is stored with WAL.

Once the MemStore fills up, data is flushed into HFile. The use of WAL ensures durability in the sense that if the MemStore goes down, you will lose all metadata. WAL maintains a copy of this data for failure recovery. Every write operation is deemed completed only once a confirmation is received from both MemStore and WAL. The block diagram for write operation is shown in Fig. 7.3.

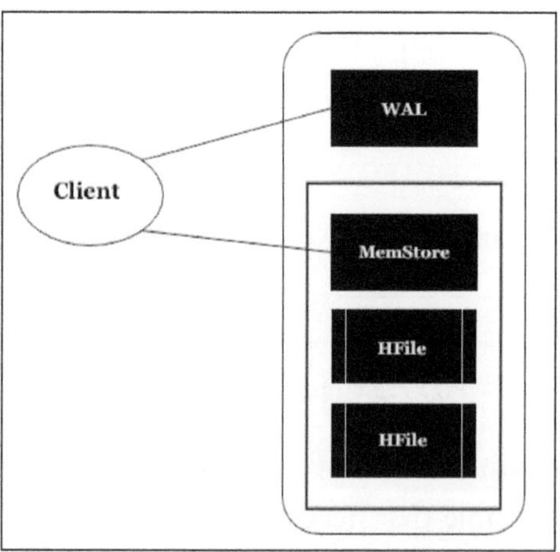

Fig. 7.3 Block Diagram – Write Operation

It is important to mention that every time the MemStore gets filled up to its capacity, a new HFile is created and all the data of MemStore is flushed out to this HFile. Therefore, multiple HFiles are created on the disk.

7.7.2 Reading Data From HBase

Whenever data needs to be read from HBase, the system tries to fulfill the demand from MemStore. However, in case that is not possible, the second point of contact is BlockCache. In case data is not available in both BlockCache and MemStore, HBase will read the HFiles on the disk. The block diagram for read operation is shown in Fig. 7.4.

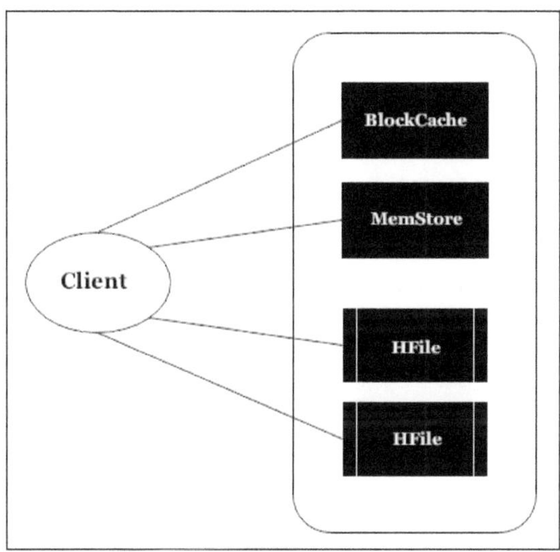

Fig. 7.4 Block Diagram – Read Operation

7.7.3 Compaction of HFiles

Since MemStore creates small HFiles on the disk, a consolidation scheme for these files is also present, which is known as compaction. HBase allows two types of compaction namely major compaction and minor compaction. Two or more HFiles can be combined to form a single HFile, which is referred to as 'Compacted HFile,' as shown in Fig. 7.5.

Major compaction allows dropping of deleted and duplicate or older versions of records while minor compaction just performs consolidation on the basis of a heuristic. It is crucial to understand that deleted records are just marked as deleted and exist in the form of their corresponding HFiles. These deleted records are actually removed only once major compaction is performed.

7.8 HBASE STORAGE ARCHITECTURE

The three main components of HBase architecture are HBaseMaster, HRegionServer and HBaseClient. The HBaseMaster manages the HBase cluster and is connected to all the HRegionServers. Each HRegionServer has two sub-components namely HLog and HRegion. HLog keeps track of all the edits made by the client in the HBase table. HRegion, on the other hand, contains MemStore and HFile for data storage. Both these sub-components use HDFS for actual storage and interact with the same using DFS Clients. WAL is located on the disk, say on the DataNodes. The default size of HRegion is 256 MB. However, editing the hbase.hregion.max.filesize parameter in Hbase-site.xml can change it. The upper limit of this parameter is 4 GB.

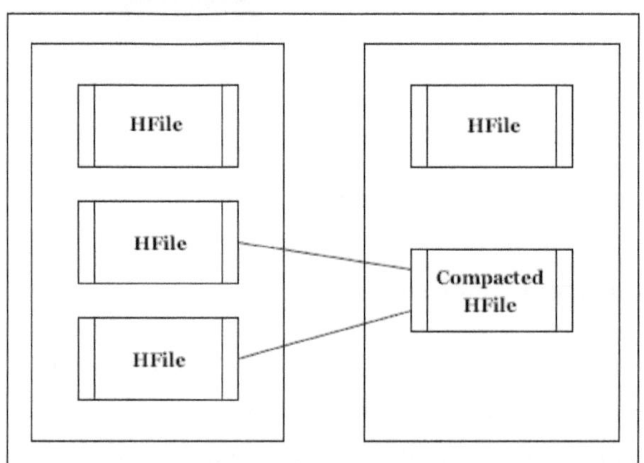

Fig. 7.5 Block Diagram – HFile Compaction

Simply, the master node will have daemons running for ZooKeeper and HBaseMaster/HDFS NameNode/HDFS Secondary NameNode and the slave will have daemons running for ZooKeeper and HBaseRegionServer. Fig. 7.6 illustrates the architecture.

7.9 NEED FOR ZOOKEEPER

Zookeeper is basically a coordination engine and serves the following purposes –

- Allows handling of complex distributed algorithms
- Avoid complexities related to management
- Avoid deadlocks and race conditions
- Allows developer to use reusable code in use-cases, simplifying the programming phase.

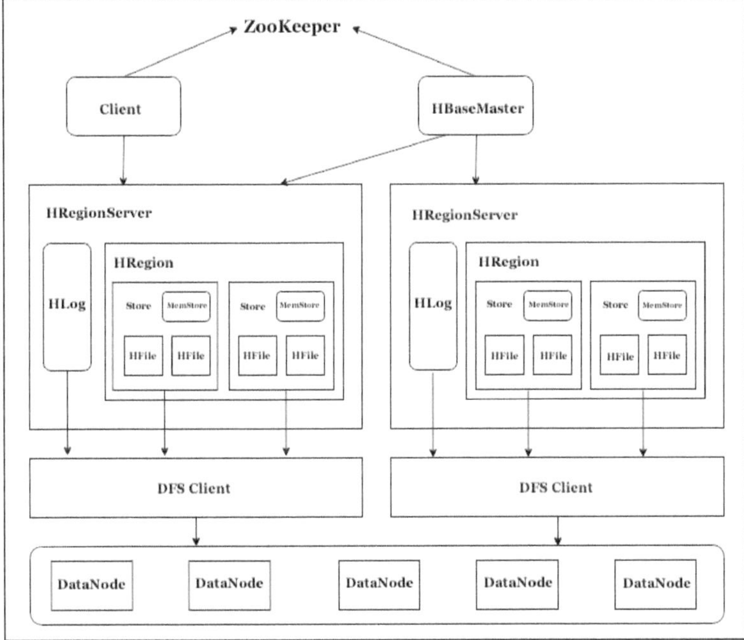

Fig. 7.6 HBase Storage Architecture

7.10 WORKING IN HBASE

HBase creates tables with the following hierarchy: rowkey, column_family, columns and data. Rowkeys must be unique and identifies a row in the table. Columns are grouped together into column families. Lastly, data is inserted into columns of a row. The data shown below will help you understand this hierarchy in a better way. Versions of data are internally maintained. However, when you view a table, you will only see the latest version. To access data, you need to follow the given hierarchy:

Table -> rowkey -> column_family -> column -> timestamp

The numbers that you see before data, in the data, are timestamps.

Rowkey	*column family*	*column*	*data*
student1			
	studentdetails		
		name	1329088341278 : “abc”
		Course	1329088341278 : “mca”
		Gender	1329088341278 : “male”
	fellowshipdetails		
		Organization	1329088341278 : “comp”
student2			
	studentdetails		
		Name	1329088341376 : “abc”
		course	1329088341376 : “bca”
		gender	1329088345674 : “female”
			1329088341376 : “male”

As far as data storage is concerned, HBase sorts and stores the columns in a family together. Any number of columns can be stored. By default, three versions of data are stored. However, this can be changed.

7.10.1 Java Client API

HBase offers both command line interface and Java API for accessing it. The HTable package in Java is:

org.apache.hadoop.hbase.client.Htable

This client API can be used to perform varied operations in HBase. The interfaces available include –

- HTable
  It is a handle for a single table and allows operations to be performed on the table.
- HBaseDescriptor
  It contains table details.
- HBaseAdmin
  This interface is responsible for management of administrative tasks.
- Configuration
  This interface allows the developer to access cluster setting and tune the same according to the requirements of the system.

7.10.2 Data Loading Techniques

Data can be loaded into HBase using one of the following tools –

- Sqoop
- Client API
- Pig
- HBase Shell

OBJECTIVE-TYPE QUESTIONS

1. Which of these is an HBase feature?

   a. Support for sparse data
   b. Distributed database
   c. Multi-dimensional data storage
   d. All of the above

2. Which of these systems support variable schema?

   a. HBase
   b. RDBMS
   c. Both a and b
   d. Neither a nor b

3. Which of these HBase components maintains a log of edits made to the HBase table?

   a. HLog
   b. Write Ahead Log (WAL)
   c. MemStore
   d. None of the above

4. Which of these components is responsible for performing coordination activities?

   a. NodeManager
   b. ResourceManager
   c. ZooKeeper
   d. HBaseMaster

SHORT ANSWER QUESTIONS

1. HBase falls under which class of NoSQL databases and why? Also explain how this class of NoSQL databases is different from the other classes.
2. Explain how HBase handles NULL values in sparse tables? Also, elaborate on whether the NULL value entries are visible to the user if he or she performs a scan of the table?
3. List the three main components of HBase and discuss the functions of each of them?

LONG ANSWER QUESTIONS

1. Explain CAP theorem. Elaborate on how and where HBase is located on the CAP triangle.
2. What are the key requirements of big data applications? How does HBase meet these requirements?
3. Discuss the HBase storage architecture elaborating on how read and write operations are made in HBase?

Chapter 8

OOZIE

OBJECTIVES

- Basic concepts of Oozie
- Scheduling jobs in Oozie
- Understanding Oozie Workflow
- Understanding Oozie Coordinator

8.1 UNDERSTANDING OOZIE

Given a problem statement, you might be required to put all the different components that we have studied so far into a chain to define an automated workflow to solve your problem. Oozie enables you to do this by allowing you to define the set of tasks that need to be executed to solve a specific problem. So, when you have a new dataset that needs the same processing, you can reuse the defined workflow.

In other words, Oozie is a coordination system that can be used for management of Hadoop jobs. It is currently in use by Yahoo! It contains an Oozie server, which is a web application running on a Java servlet container. When you run this application, you are provided with an interface, which you can use for managing Hadoop jobs. The workflows can be read and executed by the server.

Besides this, it also has definitions for coordinators and bundles. Coordinators and bundle definitions allow you to automate the execution flow. This automation is defined in three steps –

1. Define the workflow in HPDL, which is a process defining language used by Oozie.
2. This workflow is given to the coordinator, which provides automated execution. For example, you can tell the coordinator to start execution when the data is available or at any time you want.
3. Bundle packages the whole thing for a working job, making it easy for you to manage jobs.

The main features of Oozie include –

- Execution and monitoring of workflows in Hadoop
- Allows triggering of workflow execution on the basis of data availability
- Allows periodic scheduling of workflows
- Provides HTTP, command line and web interface

8.2 FUNCTIONAL COMPONENTS OF OOZIE

There are three functional components of Oozie namely Workflow, Coordinator and Bundles. A workflow may contain a controlled sequence of jobs, which may include MapReduce, Hive and Pig jobs. This component allows the developer to define and execute workflows.

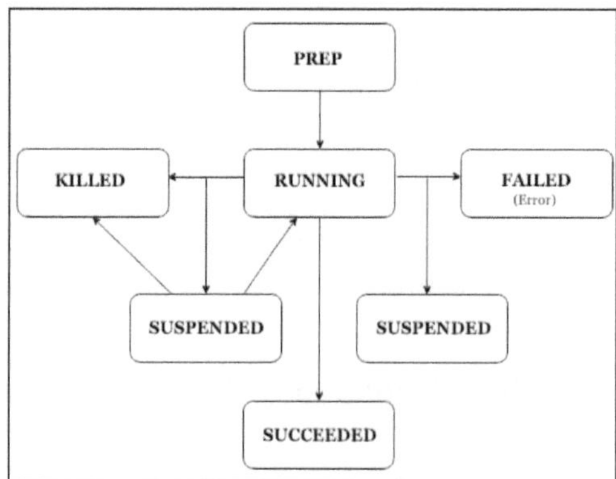

Fig. 8.1 State Diagram

On the basis of time and data availability, automatic execution of jobs can be executed with the help of Oozie coordinator. It packages multiple workflow and coordinator jobs together. Therefore, it makes it easier for the developer to manage the lifecycle of these jobs.

8.2.1 Oozie Workflow

A workflow job can be in one of the following states: PREP, RUNNING and SUSPENDED. When you create a workflow job, it is initially in PREP state. In fact, it remains in PREP state until the job starts running. When the job starts executing, its state changes to RUNNING and remains in this state until it ends with the required result, ends with an error or is suspended. Once a running job is suspended, it is either killed or it goes back to the running state. The state diagram is illustrated in Fig. 8.1. You can view the state of your jobs in the Oozie web interface and take necessary actions. For instance, if a job has failed, you can check why the job has failed.

8.2.2 Scheduling with Oozie

Whenever you want to run a MapReduce/Pig/Hive job using Oozie, it must be given to the Oozie Coordinator and the coordinator runs the job as per the time and data instruction given. The execution of the job is similar to a normal MapReduce job. Oozie uses an XML-based process definition language called HPDL (Hadoop Process Definition Language). To give the job to Oozie, you need to at least give a name, starting point and end point to the workflow by creating a file called workflow.xml and adding following content to it.

```
<workflow-app xmlns="uri:oozie:workflow:0.1"
name="WorkflowRunnerTest">
        <start to="process1"/>
        <end name="end"/>
>/workflow-app>
```

The start node specifies the starting point for an Oozie workflow while end node specifies where the workflow will end. Flow control nodes control the execution path of the workflow. To the basic code given above, we add an action. Actions require <Ok> and <error> tags to tell the coordinator what to do upon success or failure of the job. If you wish to run a MapReduce job, the action for workflow.xml file would be as follows –

```
<action name="process1">
<map-reduce>
<job-tracker>localhost:8032</job-tracker>
<name-node>hdfs://localhost:9000</name-node>
<prepare><delete
path="hdfs://localhost:9000/Test/out1/></prepare>
<configuration>
<property>
<name>mapred.input.dir</name>
<value>${inputDir}</value>
</property>
<property>
<name>mapred.output.dir</name>
<value>${outputDir}</value>
</property>
</configuration>
</map-reduce>
<ok to="end"/>
<error to="fall"/>
</action>
```

The job that needs to be executed is taken from the properties file. Therefore, job.properties file includes all the arguments for the job. The libraries that are required for Oozie workflow execution are included in the lib directory. Files that are usually included entail JAR files and Shared Object (SO) Files. For Oozie, you can keep the properties file local while you can push everything else like the JAR file to be executed and the data input to HDFS.

8.2.3 Oozie Coordinator

Oozie workflow processes can be automatically started with the help of the Oozie Coordinator. This component is typically used for invoking execution of workflow processes on a recurrent basis depending on the time and data requirements set by the user. The parameters for the coordinator are set in a properties or xml file. The variables used for setting data and time settings are $inputDir and $startTime. The values of these variables must be provided in the xml or properties file while submitting a coordinator job. The manner in which these variables are given in the xml file is shown below –

```
<coordinator-app name="coord_1">
start="2017-07-02T00\:00Z"
end="2017-07-03T00\:00Z"
frequency="60"
<action>
<workflow>
<app-path>hdfs://localhost:9000/TestApp</app-path>
<configuration>
<property><name>key123</name><value>value123</value></
property>
</configuration>
</workflow>
</action>
</coordinator-app>
```

In this sample xml file, frequency is specified as 60, which means that the coordinator will run the application every hour. The start and end times state the date and time from which the coordinator will initiate and terminate execution respectively. Such a use case works on time triggers. Now, let us see how we can make the coordinator run an application only when the input data for the same is available. For this, the xml file will look something like this:

```
<coordinator-app name="coord_1" frequency="${1*HOURS}"...>
<datasets>
<dataset name="logs" frequency="${1*HOURS}" initial-
instance="2017-07-02T00\:00Z">
<uri-template>hdfs://bar:9000/app/
logs/${YEAR}/${MONTH}/${DAY}/
</datasets>
<input-events>
<data-in name="inputLogs" dataset="logs">
<instance>${current(0)}</instance>
</data-in>
</input-events>
<action>
<workflow>
<app-path>hdfs://localhost:9000/TestApp</app-path>
<configuration>
<property><name>inputData</
name><value>${dataIn('inputLogs')}</value></property>
</configuration>
</workflow>
</action>
</coordinator-app>
```

With this coordinator configuration, the coordinator will go and look at the path specified in uri-template, every hour. If the data file is available, it will execute the application, else it will come back again after 1 hour to check for data availability.

Alternatively, you can also set the rolling time window in which the coordinator shall run a job every 15 minutes (for example) for the first 5 hours (for example) and then change the repetition duration to 30 minutes (for example) for the rest of the time period.

OBJECTIVE-TYPE QUESTIONS

1. Workflows are defined in Oozie using which of the following languages?
    a. HPDL (Hadoop Process Definition Language)
    b. HiveQL
    c. Pig Latin
    d. None of the above
2. Which of these triggers for job initiation can be managed using Coordinator component of Oozie?
    a. Data triggers
    b. Time triggers
    c. Both a and b
    d. Neither a nor b
3. Which types of jobs can be run using Oozie?
    a. Pig
    b. Hive
    c. MapReduce
    d. All of the above

SHORT ANSWER QUESTIONS

1. Explain the main function of Oozie? Also, elaborate on the key features of Oozie?
2. What is a workflow? Explain with the help of an example?
3. List the three steps involved in running a workflow with the help of Oozie?

LONG ANSWER QUESTIONS

1. List the different states in which a job can be in, while in Oozie? Also draw the state diagram to explain the transition between the states?
2. What are the different components of Oozie? Explain the functions of each of the components in detail?

Chapter 9

INTEGRATING R WITH HADOOP

OBJECTIVES

- Understand the use of R programming language and improvements that it provides upon integration with Hadoop.
- Learn the different integration methods used for integrating R programming language with Hadoop.
- Realize the advantages and disadvantages of using the different integration methods.

9.1 INTRODUCTION TO R

Pig and Hive are the key abstraction tools when it comes to big data analytics. However, when faced with scenarios that require mathematical and statistical data analysis for Hadoop and big data sources, the programming language of choice for most data analysts and scientists is R. The fundamental reason behind the popularity of R programming language is its rich ecosystem, which provides tools for performing correlation, data analysis and preparation.

Hadoop and R are not inherently complementary. However, with the advent of packages like RHIPE, RHIVE and RHadoop, these two technologies can be seamlessly integrated to work together. While Hadoop is a framework that allows cost-effective storage and processing of big data,

R provides packages for statistical analysis and visualization of the same. Together, these two technologies form a good big data ecosystem.

There are several ways in which R and Hadoop can be integrated and there is always a question raised on what are the factors on the basis of which the integration method must be chosen. In this chapter, we shall give you an overview of these factors involved in development of a scalable, performance-effective and stable solution.

9.2 USING R WITH HADOOP

R is basically a data science tool that is used on models to perform statistical analysis. Besides this, R can also be used to create visualizations. However, the biggest shortcoming of R framework is its inability to cater to large datasets.

The reason for this is the fact that R requires loading of all objects in the machine's main memory. This is not practically possible with datasets that are of the size of petabytes. This limitation is existent owing to the fact that R is not a scalable programming language and the core R engine has limits when it comes to the size of dataset that it can process.

Looking at the one-machine, in-memory executions of R, most data scientists take a sample of data from big dataset and use the same to perform analysis. They extrapolate the result to fit into the big data scenario. However, this approach limits the accuracy and effectiveness of the analysis.

Hadoop solves this problem and this is why Hadoop and R make an ideal data analytics solution for big data. Hadoop is a distributed programming framework, which is highly scalable and is designed to process large datasets in a performance-effective manner. However, Hadoop lacks the strong statistical tools and packages available in R.

This logical approach leads to integration of Hadoop and R. Integrating R with Hadoop shall provide for scalable data analytics, which is one of the fundamental requirements of big data. Hadoop allows the statistical tools available in R to run in parallel for large datasets.

9.3 INTEGRATION METHODS FOR R AND HADOOP

R has a rich library with packages for any kind of data processing that the day-to-day job of a data scientist requires. However, if you are using just Hadoop, then the data scientist is required to rewrite the R code into Java or any programming language that implements MapReduce for the program to become executable in the Hadoop environment. This is a laborious and time-consuming task. Moreover, it is not even required. In order to integrate R with Hadoop, the code for analysis needs to be written in R and the data must be stored in Hadoop. Some of the standard methods used for integrating these two technologies are discussed below.

9.3.1 RHadoop

In this kind of a setup, R is installed on the workstations and data is available in Hadoop. Therefore, the system connects with Hadoop to access data. An organization named Revolution Analytics developed this solution and it works on the base principle that supports direct ingestion of data from HBase and HDFS into the R ecosystem. The simplicity and cost-effectiveness of this model makes it one of the best available solutions for R and Hadoop integration.

RHadoop includes five packages that are used for management and analysis of data using R. Moreover, this package is compatible with almost all versions of Hadoop including the open-source version, Cloudera, MapR and Hortonworks. The five packages included in RHadoop are as follows –

- *rhbase*
  This package allows interaction of the R client with data available in HBase. Using this package, Hbase tables can be read, written and modified within the R environment. All the database management functions supported by this package make use of Thrift Server.
- *rhdfs*
  This package supports accessibility of HDFS for reading, writing and modifying data present in it from within the R programming environment.

- *plyrmr*

  The plyr package is a package that provides tools for splitting, applying and combining data. The plyrmr package is basically plyr for MapReduce and is used for manipulating large datasets that are available in Hadoop. Operations available in popular packages like plyr and reshape2 can be used through this package. It is important to mention that although this package abstracts most of the MapReduce details for performing operations, the package is dependent on MapReduce for performing these operations.
- *ravro*

  This package supports reading and writing of AVRO from HDFS as well as local file system.
- *rmr2*

  This package is used for executing R programs inside the Hadoop MapReduce framework. This is the case when the dataset is stored in the Hadoop cluster and statistical analysis needs to be performed on this data using R code. Even though this process is a tiresome task, but it is usually preferred over the actual MapReduce implementation.

9.3.2 RHIPE

RHIPE stands for R and Hadoop Integrated Programming Environment, which is a library in R. Using this library, users can execute MapReduce tasks from within the R programming environment. As part of this method, the developer is expected to write R map and R reduce tasks. The *RHIPE* library maps these tasks to their corresponding Hadoop Map and Hadoop Reduce tasks and executes the same.

For mapping of map and reduce tasks, *RHIPE* makes use of a protocol buffer encoding scheme. The advantages of using *RHIPE* over other packages available for R integration with Hadoop is that it provides seamless integration, providing a performance effective and fault tolerant HDFS-based data distribution scheme.

9.3.3 R and Hadoop Streaming

Hadoop Streaming API provides users an executable script, which can be used for running MapReduce jobs. This script performs reading of data from the standard input and writes data as the mapper and reducer to the standard output. This allows users to use Hadoop Streaming API with R scripts for performing Hadoop-related functionalities.

There is no client-side integration requirement as jobs are directly launched from the command line of Hadoop. It is important to note that MapReduce jobs need to undergo data transformation to ensure that they comply with the standards of Java input that Hadoop requires. This takes place irrespective of the language of the script given by the developer.

9.3.4 RHIVE

In this method, R programming environment is installed on all the client systems and the clients access the data, which is available on the Hadoop ecosystem. *RHIVE* is a package that allows you to run Hive queries from within the R programming environment. In addition to providing standard functions for retrieval of table, column and database names, *RHIVE* also extends the functionality of Hive by providing it a list of statistical functions that can be applied on the data available in Hive tables. The advantage of using this method is that the operations are parallelized without initiating any substantial data movement.

9.4 SOLVING PROBLEMS WITH R AND HADOOP

The combination of Hadoop and R is the best solution for developing applications for predictive analytics that are required to be fast, scalable and performance-effective. This makes R and Hadoop a must-have in the toolkit of all data scientists and analytics professionals. Standalone, each of these technologies falls short in meeting the challenges posed by big data analytics.

While Hadoop lacks the statistical libraries and functions to perform complex analysis and visualization of data, R is non-distributed in nature;

as a result of which data retrieval is time consuming and the response time of the application suffers. Together, they are the best that any analytics professional might require.

Although, there are a plethora of options available in the market that claim to perform big data analytics with Hadoop and R, the list of solutions given in this chapter still remain the best of the best.

OBJECTIVE-TYPE QUESTIONS

1. Which of these is a package of RHadoop?

   a. rhbase
   b. rhdfs
   c. rmr2
   d. All of the above

2. Which of these is a limitation of R that makes it necessary to integrate it with Hadoop?

   a. Lack of statistical functions
   b. In-memory processing
   c. Large data retrieval time
   d. Both b and c

SHORT ANSWER QUESTIONS

1. List the packages that are included in RHadoop. Also, describe the function of each package.
2. Describe the two advantages of R, which makes it a good tool for big data analytics.

LONG ANSWER QUESTIONS

1. Describe the limitations of both Hadoop and R in meeting the demands of big data applications? Also, explain how the synergistic approach of using Hadoop and R can solve the big data problem effectively?

Chapter 10

SETTING UP HADOOP STANDALONE CLUSTER

Hadoop can be installed in two ways, single-node cluster or standalone cluster mode and multi-node cluster mode. Standalone clusters run the master and slave daemons on the same machine and are usually used for development and testing purposes. On the other hand, multi-node clusters have more than one node, with master and slaves running of different systems. This lab tutorial covers the installation of Hadoop (Standalone mode) on Ubuntu.

Step 1:

A prerequisite of installing Hadoop is Java 8 package. You can download the Java 8 package and install it before starting with Hadoop installation.

Step 2:

Secondly, you need to download the tar file for Hadoop and extract its contents. Remember to change your directory to home directory before starting this step using command cd.

> *wget https://archive.apache.org/dist/hadoop/core/hadoop-2.7.3/hadoop-2.7.3.tar.gz*
> *tar -xvf hadoop-2.7.3.tar.gz*

Step 3:

To inform the system about the changes, .bashrc file needs to be edited. For this, you need to open the file in editing mode using the command:

gedit .bashrc

Add the following lines to the file:

```
#Set Hadoop Paths
export HADOOP_HOME=$HOME/hadoop-2.7.3
export HADOOP_CONF_DIR=$HOME/hadoop-2.7.3/etc/hadoop
export HADOOP_MAPRED_HOME=$HOME/hadoop-2.7.3
export HADOOP_COMMON_HOME=$HOME/hadoop-2.7.3
export HADOOP_HDFS_HOME=$HOME/hadoop-2.7.3
export YARN_HOME=$HOME/hadoop-2.7.3
export PATH=$PATH:$HOME/hadoop-2.7.3/bin
#Set Java Paths
export JAVA_HOME=$HOME/jdk1.8.0_101
export PATH=$HOME/jdk1.8.0_101/bin:$PATH
```

To apply the changes made, execute the following command:

source .bashrc

Step 4:

Before moving forward, check if all is good so far by running the following commands and checking if they are giving valid results.

```
java -version
hadoop version
```

Step 5:

Now that java and Hadoop are installed, it is time to edit the Hadoop configuration files. For this, you need to first change the directory using the following command:

cd hadoop-2.7.3/etc/hadoop/

Step 6:

Now open the file core-site.xml in editing mode using the command:

gedit core-site.xml

Add the property as shown in the text below:

```
<?xml version="1.0" encoding="UTF-8"?>
<?xml-stylesheet type="text/xsl" href="configuration.xsl"?>
<configuration>
<property>
<name>fs.default.name</name>
<value>hdfs://localhost:9000</value>
</property>
</configuration>
```

Step 7:

Open the file hdfs-site.xml in editing mode using the command:

gedit hdfs-site.xml

Add the property as shown in the text below:

```
<?xml version="1.0" encoding="UTF-8"?>
<?xml-stylesheet type="text/xsl" href="configuration.xsl"?>
<configuration>
<property>
<name>dfs.replication</name>
<value>1</value>
</property>
<property>
<name>dfs.permission</name>
<value>false</value>
</property>
</configuration>
```

Step 8:

Open the file mapred-site.xml in editing mode using the command:

```
gedit mapred-site.xml
```

If the file is not present, run the following command before gedit:

```
cp mapred-site.xml.template mapred-site.xml
```

Add the property as shown in the text below:

```
<?xml version="1.0" encoding="UTF-8"?>
<?xml-stylesheet type="text/xsl" href="configuration.xsl"?>
<configuration>
<property>
<name>mapreduce.framework.name</name>
<value>yarn</value>
</property>
</configuration>
```

Step 9:

Open the file yarn-site.xml in editing mode using the command:

```
gedit yarn-site.xml
```

Add the property as shown in the text below:

```
<?xml version="1.0">
<configuration>
<property>
<name>yarn.nodemanager.aux-services</name>
<value>mapreduce_shuffle</value>
</property>
<property>
<name>yarn.nodemanager.auxservices.mapreduce.shuffle.class</
name>
<value>org.apache.hadoop.mapred.ShuffleHandler</value>
```

</property>
</configuration>

Step 10:

Finally edit the hadoop-env.sh file. For this, you will need to open the file in editing mode using the command:

gedit hadoop-env.sh

Add the following lines to the file:

#Set Java Path
export JAVA_HOME=$HOME/jdk1.8.0_101

Step 11:

Now that you are all set to work in Hadoop, there are a couple of things that you will have to do.

1. Change directory to hadoop
   cd hadoop-2.7.3
2. Format NameNode
   bin/hadoop namenode -format
3. Change directory to sbin
   cd hadoop-2.7.3/sbin
4. Start services
   a. Start NameNode
      ./hadoop-daemon.sh start namenode
   b. Start DataNode
      ./hadoop-daemon.sh start datanode
   c. Start ResourceManager
      ./yarn-daemon.sh start resourcemanager
   d. Start NodeManager
      ./yarn-daemon.sh start nodemanager
   e. Start JobHistoryServer
      ./mr-jobhistory-daemon.sh start historyserver

Step 12:

Check if Hadoop is working with the help of following steps.

1. Check if all daemons are working.
   jps
2. Open the following link on the browser to check if the interface is working.
   localhost:50070/dfshealth.html

Chapter 11

SETTING UP HADOOP MULTI-NODE CLUSTER

To set up a multi-node cluster, let us take two machines: one for the master and other for the slave. To install Hadoop (multi-node) on Ubuntu, you need to follow the steps given below.

Step 1:

Check the IP address of the two machines using the command:

ip addr show

Step 2:

The next step requires you to disable firewall restrictions. For this, you will need to run the following commands:

service iptables stop
sudo chkconfig iptables off

Step 3:

Add the master and slave IP addresses to the hosts file on both the machines. For this you will need to open the file in editing mode using the command:

sudo nano /etc/hosts

Add the following lines to the file:

192.168.56.102 master
192.168.56.103 slave

Assuming that the IP addresses of the master and slave are as provided above.

Step 4:

Restart the sshd service using the command:

service sshd restart

Step 5:

In the master machine, create the SSH key using the command:

ssh-keygen -t rsa -P ""

This generated key needs to be copied to the authorized keys for the master node and slave node. For this, you need to give the following command on master node:

cat $HOME/.ssh/id_rsa.pub >> $HOME/.ssh/authorized_keys

You also need to give the following command on slave node:

ssh-copy-id -i $HOME/.ssh/id_rsa.pub keys@slave

Step 6:

Follow the installation steps given for Hadoop (Standalone) on both the nodes.

Step 7:

Now, start all the daemons for the master and slave and run the following commands:

On master –

jps

On slave –

jps slave

Finally, open the following link in the browser:

On master –

master:50070/dfshealth.html

You should be able to see 2 live nodes if you scroll down on the page.

Chapter 12

BASIC HDFS COMMANDS

SUDO JPS

Checks if all the daemons are working.

sudo jps

In case any of the daemons are not running, the following commands must be performed.

sudo service hadoop-master stop
sudo service hadoop-master start
hadoop dfsadmin -safemode leave
sudo jps

VERSION COMMAND

Checks the version of hadoop running on the system.

hadoop version

LS COMMAND

Lists the files on the system directory.

hadoop dfs –ls /

MKDIR COMMAND

Creates a directory in the specified location.

hdfs dfs –mkdir /directory_name

Example:

hdfs dfs –mkdir /sample
hadoop dfs –ls /

TOUCHZ COMMAND

Create a 0 byte size file

hdfs dfs –touchz /directory/filename

Example:

hdfs dfs –touchz /sample/sample_file

DU COMMAND

Check filesize

hdfs dfs –du –s /path/to/file_in_hdfs

Example:

hdfs dfs –du –s /sample /sample_file_1

COPYFROMLOCAL COMMAND

Copy the file from Local file system to HDFS.

hdfs fs -copyFromLocal <localsrc> URI

Example:

hdfs dfs –copyFromLocal /home/Desktop/test /sample

COPYTOLOCAL COMMAND

Copy the file to Local file system from HDFS.

hdfs fs -copyToLocal URI <localdst>

Example:

hdfs dfs –copyToLocal /sample/test /home/Desktop

PUT COMMAND

Copy single source, or multiple srcs from local file system to the destination file system.

hdfs fs -put <localsrc> ... <dst>

Example:

hdfs dfs –put /home/Desktop/test /user

GET COMMAND

Copy files from hdfs to the local file system.

hadoop fs -get [-ignorecrc] [-crc] <src> <localdst>

Example:

hdfs dfs –get /user/test /home/Desktop

Note: copyToLocal and copyFromLocal is similar to get and put command, except that the destination is restricted to a local file reference.

CAT COMMAND

Copies source path to stdout

hdfs dfs –cat /path/to/file_in_hdfs

Example:

hdfs dfs –cat /sample/test

TEXT COMMAND

Another command for CAT

hdfs dfs –text /path/to/file_in_hdfs

Example:

hdfs dfs –text /sample/test

COUNT COMMAND

Count the number of directories, files and bytes under the paths that match the specified file pattern.

hdfs dfs –count /user

RM COMMAND

Remove the file from HDFS.

hdfs dfs –rm /path/to/file_in_hdfs

Example:

hdfs dfs –rm /sample/test

RMR COMMAND

Remove the directory from HDFS

hdfs dfs –rmr /path/to/directory_in_hdfs

Example:

hdfs dfs –rmr /sample/

NOTE –

To create a new file in local filesystem, you can use gedit or vi commands.

gedit <filename>

Chapter 13

WRITING AND EXECUTING MAPREDUCE PROGRAMS

RUNNING A MAPREDUCE JOB IN HADOOP

To execute a MapReduce code on Hadoop, you need to follow these steps –

1. Create a Java Project in Eclipse
2. Create a .java file or copy the java code already created into the project
3. To get rid of errors coming due to lack of definitions, 'configure buildpath' for the project source. Add both common and MapReduce libraries.
4. Create a jar file for the project (right click on the source to find export, export as jar file, mention the main class to use).
5. By the end of the process explained above, you will have the jar file with you. For easier understanding, copy the jar file and input to the Desktop.
6. Open the terminal and type 'sudo jps' to check if all the daemons are running. The output must show ResourceManager, NodeManager, NameNode, DataNode and JPS. If any of the daemons are missing, you can run the following commands and re-run the sudo jps command.

   sudo service hadoop-master stop

sudo service hadoop-master start

7. Check if the data and jar file exist on the Desktop by entering the Desktop directory from the terminal and doing ls. Please note that you should be in the Desktop directory to run this command.
8. Copy the data file into the Hadoop cluster using the following command:

    hadoop dfs copyFromLocal /home/user/Desktop/A.txt hdfs:/
9. Please note that you need to provide the absolute path of the source file.
10. Before moving on, check if the file has been successfully copied by giving the following command:

    hadoop fs -ls /
11. Run the jar file 'sp_1.jar' with input file hdfs:/A.txt and output directory hdfs:/sp1_out (this directory must not exist)

    hadoop jar sp_1.jar hdfs:/A.txt hdfs:/sp1_out
12. Check if the output directory has been created.

    hadoop fs -ls /
13. Check the contents of the output directory

    hadoop fs -ls /sp1_out
14. To check the contents of the output file, open Mozilla and give the following URL:

    http://localhost:50070/dfshealth.jsp

    Click the link -> Go to File System -> sp1_out

    Check the contents of the part file to see the output

MAPREDUCE PROGRAMMING EXERCISES

1. Calculate the frequency of occurrence of each word.

    Example:

    Sample File –

    This is summer I am xyz

    I am xyz

    This is summer

    Output for the given file:

    This 2

is	2
summer	2
I	2
am	2
xyz	2

2. Calculate the frequency of occurrence of words on the basis of size.

   Example:

   Sample File –

   This is summer I am xyz
   I am xyz
   This is summer

   Output for the given file:

1	2
2	4
3	2
4	2
7	2

Chapter 14

ADVANCED PROGRAMMING IN MAPREDUCE

IMPLEMENTING THE CUSTOM PARTITIONER AND COMBINER

There are two main tasks that need to be performed when implementing the custom partitioner. However, the main task is to send matching (key, value) pairs to reducers. The steps involved in this process are –

1. Configure Hadoop job to use partitioner.
2. Use GetPartition to get a number for getting the number of reducers that the Hadoop job requires. Moreover, this logic explicitly defines which output will go to which reducer for processing. Sample code for the same can be found below.

Key changes in the MapReduce program have been described and explained below.

The number of reducers can be set using the configuration setting –

conf.setNumReduceTasks(<number>)

In this case, the combiner works on the same logic as the reducer. Therefore, combiner class is set in the following manner –

```
conf.setCombinerClass(Reduce.class);
```

However, this can be changed as per the requirements of the application.

The partitioner class is set in the following manner –

```
conf.setPartitionerClass(MyPartitioner.class)
```

This statement tells the system that custom partitioner logic has been implemented. In the absence of this statement, system assumes that the default partitioning logic needs to be executed.

The revised program will look like this –

```
import java.io.IOException;
import java.util.Iterator;
import java.util.StringTokenizer;
import org.apache.hadoop.fs.Path;
import org.apache.hadoop.io.IntWritable;
import org.apache.hadoop.io.LongWritable;
import org.apache.hadoop.io.Text;
import org.apache.hadoop.mapred.FileInputFormat;
import org.apache.hadoop.mapred.FileOutputFormat;
import org.apache.hadoop.mapred.JobClient;
import org.apache.hadoop.mapred.JobConf;
import org.apache.hadoop.mapred.MapReduceBase;
import org.apache.hadoop.mapred.Mapper;
import org.apache.hadoop.mapred.OutputCollector;
import org.apache.hadoop.mapred.Partitioner;
import org.apache.hadoop.mapred.Reducer;
import org.apache.hadoop.mapred.Reporter;
import org.apache.hadoop.mapred.TextInputFormat;
import org.apache.hadoop.mapred.TextOutputFormat;
```

```
//The name of the file must be the same as the name of this class (WithPartitioner.
class)

        public class WithPartitioner {
        //The Map Function
                public static class Map extends MapReduceBase implements
                                Mapper<LongWritable, Text, Text,
                                IntWritable> {
                        @Override
                        public void map(LongWritable key, Text value,
                                OutputCollector<Text, IntWritable> output,
                                Reporter reporter)
                                throws IOException {
                                String line = value.toString();
                                StringTokenizer tokenizer = new
                                StringTokenizer(line);
                                while (tokenizer.hasMoreTokens()) {
                                        value.set(tokenizer.nextToken());
                                        output.collect(value, new
                                        IntWritable(1));
                                }
                        }
                }

//This class implements the custom partitioner logic
        public static class MyPartitioner implements Partitioner<Text,
        IntWritable> {
                @Override
                public int getPartition(Text key, IntWritable value, int
                numPartitions) {
                        String myKey = key.toString().toLowerCase();
/*Sends key_value=" hadoop" to reducer 0; key_value="data" to reducer 1 and
everything else to reducer 2*/
                        if (myKey.equals("hadoop")) {
```

```
                return 0;
            }
            if (myKey.equals("data")) {
                return 1;
            } else {
                return 2;
            }
        }
        @Override
        public void configure(JobConf arg0) {
    // Gives you a new instance of JobConf if you want to change Job
            // Configurations
        }
    }
//The Reduce Function
    public static class Reduce extends MapReduceBase implements
            Reducer<Text, IntWritable, Text, IntWritable> {
        @Override
        public void reduce(Text key, Iterator<IntWritable> values,
            OutputCollector<Text, IntWritable> output,
            Reporter reporter)
            throws IOException {
            int sum = 0;
            while (values.hasNext()) {
                sum += values.next().get();
            }
            output.collect(key, new IntWritable(sum));
        }
    }
//The Main function
    public static void main(String[] args) throws Exception {
        JobConf conf = new JobConf(WithPartitioner.class);
    //Set configuration parameters
        conf.setJobName("wordcount_withPC");
```

```
            //Sets the number of reducers to 3 (reducer 0, reducer 1, reducer 2)
            conf.setNumReduceTasks(3);
            conf.setMapperClass(Map.class);
            conf.setCombinerClass(Reduce.class);
            conf.setReducerClass(Reduce.class);
            conf.setPartitionerClass(MyPartitioner.class);
            conf.setOutputKeyClass(Text.class);
            conf.setOutputValueClass(IntWritable.class);
            conf.setInputFormat(TextInputFormat.class);
            conf.setOutputFormat(TextOutputFormat.class);
    //Set input output parametets
            FileInputFormat.setInputPaths(conf, new Path(args[0]));
            FileOutputFormat.setOutputPath(conf, new Path(args[1]));
    //Instruct the system to run the job
            JobClient.runJob(conf);
    }
}
```

PERFORMING MAP SIDE JOIN IN MAPREDUCE

To implement the Map Side Join, two things need to be done. Firstly, the small dataset needs to be added to the distributed cache. It is done in the following manner –

```
DistributedCache.addCacheFile(new URI("/sample.dat"), job.
getConfiguration());
```

As a result, the file is distributed to all the nodes inside the cluster. Since the distributed cache is accessible to all the nodes of the cluster now, data is available to all the nodes, but editing this data simultaneously by multiple mappers running on different nodes may result in data inconsistency. Therefore, a local copy of the dataset must be made available to every mapper before it starts executing. This is done in the following manner –

```
Path[] files = DistributedCache.getLocalCacheFiles(context.
getConfiguration());
```

This statement creates a local copy of the files available in distributed cache.

To understand how the distributed cache can be used for performing a map side join, let us take an example. Assuming that you have two files; one containing names of states in acronym form with the corresponding full form and the other containing the population of each state with state given in the acronym form. Now, if we wish to output the name of the state, the name of the state in full form and the population statistics for the same, we will need to perform a join. Join performed using distributed cache can be implemented in the following manner.

```
import java.io.BufferedReader;
import java.io.FileReader;
import java.io.IOException;
import java.net.URI;
import java.util.HashMap;
import java.util.Map;
import org.apache.hadoop.conf.Configuration;
import org.apache.hadoop.filecache.DistributedCache;
import org.apache.hadoop.fs.Path;
import org.apache.hadoop.io.IntWritable;
import org.apache.hadoop.io.LongWritable;
import org.apache.hadoop.io.Text;
import org.apache.hadoop.mapreduce.Mapper.Context;
import org.apache.hadoop.mapreduce.lib.input.FileInputFormat;
import org.apache.hadoop.mapreduce.lib.output.FileOutputFormat;
import org.apache.hadoop.mapreduce.Counter;
import org.apache.hadoop.mapreduce.Counters;
import org.apache.hadoop.mapreduce.Job;
import org.apache.hadoop.mapreduce.Mapper;

//The name of the file must be same as the name of the class
public class MyMapJoinDistributedCache {
public static class MyMapper extends Mapper<LongWritable, Text,
Text, Text> {
```

```
        private Map<String, String> abMap = new HashMap<String,
String>();
        private Text outputKey = new Text();
        private Text outputValue = new Text();
protected void setup(Context context) throws java.io.IOException,
InterruptedException{
//Gets a local copy of the files in distributed cache
        Path[] files = DistributedCache.getLocalCacheFiles(context.
getConfiguration());
for (Path p : files) {
        //checks if the file for which a local copy has been created is the
expected file
                if (p.getName().equals("sample.dat")) {
BufferedReader reader = new BufferedReader(new FileReader(p.
toString()));
                        String line = reader.readLine();
                        while(line != null) {
                                String[] tokens = line.split("\t");
                                String ab = tokens[0];
                                String state = tokens[1];
                                abMap.put(ab, state);
                                line = reader.readLine();
                        }
                }
        }
        if (abMap.isEmpty()) {
                throw new IOException("Unable to load Abbrevation
data.");
                }
        }
        protected void map(LongWritable key, Text value, Context
        context)
        throws java.io.IOException, InterruptedException {
        String row = value.toString();
```

```
            String[] tokens = row.split("\t");
            String inab = tokens[0];
            String state = abMap.get(inab);
            outputKey.set(state);
            outputValue.set(row);
            context.write(outputKey,outputValue);
    }
    }
    public static void main(String[] args)
            throws IOException, ClassNotFoundException,
            InterruptedException {
            Job job = new Job();
             job.setJarByClass(MyMapJoinDistributedCache.class);
             job.setJobName("MapJoinDistributedCache ");
            //the number of reducers is set to 0 as processing is taking
            place at the Map Side
             job.setNumReduceTasks(0);
    try{
            //The file sample.dat is added to the distributed cache before
            mapper execution
            DistributedCache.addCacheFile(new      URI("/sample.dat"),
            job.getConfiguration());
    }catch(Exception e){
            System.out.println(e);
    }
    job.setMapperClass(MyMapper.class);
    job.setMapOutputKeyClass(Text.class);
    job.setMapOutputValueClass(Text.class);
    FileInputFormat.addInputPath(job, new Path(args[0]));
    FileOutputFormat.setOutputPath(job, new Path(args[1]));
    job.waitForCompletion(true);
    }
}
```

PERFORMING REDUCE SIDE JOIN IN MAPREDUCE

Assuming that there are two datasets containing data related to customers and transactions respectively. The customer dataset has the details about the customer and transaction dataset has the details of transactions performed by customers. Therefore, one customer may have performed many transactions and the details of the same can be found in the second table. Joining these two tables can answer many questions. For example, it can be used to determine a list of most frequent customers and the total transaction amount for them.

In order to solve such a problem, three things needs to be done, which are as follows –

1. Determine the number of times a customer has performed a transaction.
2. Determine the total amount for which a customer has performed transactions.
3. Generate a report that has this information along with the customer's name.

To perform a reduce side join, you need to perform the following tasks –

1. Two different mappers need to be created for traversing each of the two datasets and extract the required information. Therefore, Multiple Input format is used (as can be seen in the code given below).
2. The first mapper that works on the customer dataset extracts customer ID and customer name from the same.
3. The second mapper extracts customer ID and transaction amount from the transaction dataset.
4. The reducer receives all the data (from both the mappers) and aggregates the data to give the desired result.

The implementation for reduce side join is as follows –

```
        import java.io.IOException;
        import org.apache.hadoop.conf.Configuration;
        import org.apache.hadoop.fs.Path;
        import org.apache.hadoop.io.Text;
        import org.apache.hadoop.mapreduce.Job;
        import org.apache.hadoop.mapreduce.Mapper;
        import org.apache.hadoop.mapreduce.Reducer;
        import org.apache.hadoop.mapreduce.lib.input.MultipleInputs;
        import org.apache.hadoop.mapreduce.lib.input.TextInputFormat;
        import org.apache.hadoop.mapreduce.lib.output.FileOutputFormat;
//The name of the file must be same as the name of this class
        public class ReduceJoin {
        //Mapper function for processing customer dataset
                public static class CustsMapper extends
                                Mapper<Object, Text, Text, Text> {
                        public void map(Object key, Text value, Context
                        context)
                                        throws IOException,
        InterruptedException {
                                String record = value.toString();
                                String[] parts = record.split(", ");
                                context.write(new Text(parts[0]), new
                                Text("custs\t" + parts[1]));
                        }
                }
        //Mapper function for processing transaction dataset
                public static class TxnsMapper extends
                                Mapper<Object, Text, Text, Text> {
                        public void map(Object key, Text value, Context
                        context)
                                        throws IOException,
        InterruptedException {
```

```
                String record = value.toString();
                String[] parts = record.split(",");
                context.write(new Text(parts[2]), new
                Text("txns\t" + parts[3]));
        }
    }
//The reducer receives records from both the mappers and aggregates results
    public static class ReduceJoinReducer extends
                Reducer<Text, Text, Text, Text> {
        public void reduce(Text key, Iterable<Text> values,
        Context context)
                    throws IOException,
    InterruptedException {
                String name = "";
                double total = 0.0;
                int count = 0;
                for (Text t : values) {
                    String parts[] = t.toString().
                    split("\t");
                    if (parts[0].equals("txns")) {
                        count++;
                        total += Float.
                        parseFloat(parts[1]);
                    } else if (parts[0].equals("custs")) {
                        name = parts[1];
                    }
                }
                String str = String.format("%d\t%f", count,
                total);
                context.write(new Text(name), new
                Text(str));
        }
    }
```

```
//Main function implementation
        public static void main(String[] args) throws Exception {
                Configuration conf = new Configuration();
                Job job = new Job(conf, "Reduce-side join");
                job.setJarByClass(ReduceJoin.class);
                job.setReducerClass(ReduceJoinReducer.class);
                job.setOutputKeyClass(Text.class);
                job.setOutputValueClass(Text.class);
        //Accounts for the two datasets or input files that need to be
        joined
                MultipleInputs.addInputPath(job, new
                Path(args[0]),TextInputFormat.class, CustsMapper.
                class);
                MultipleInputs.addInputPath(job, new
                Path(args[1]),TextInputFormat.class, TxnsMapper.
                class);
                Path outputPath = new Path(args[2]);
                FileOutputFormat.setOutputPath(job, outputPath);
                outputPath.getFileSystem(conf).delete(outputPath);
                System.exit(job.waitForCompletion(true) ? 0 : 1);
        }
}
```

IMPLEMENTATION OF COUNTERS

To understand how counters can be implemented for generating custom metrics, let us take an example. Consider a dataset containing logs. You can determine the number of log entries for each month using a simple code, as shown below. This counter implementation allows you to identify busy months. The implementation for this counter is provided below.

```
import java.io.IOException;
import java.util.Date;
import org.apache.hadoop.fs.Path;
import org.apache.hadoop.io.IntWritable;
```

```
import org.apache.hadoop.io.LongWritable;
import org.apache.hadoop.io.Text;
import org.apache.hadoop.mapreduce.Mapper.Context;
import org.apache.hadoop.mapreduce.lib.input.FileInputFormat;
import org.apache.hadoop.mapreduce.lib.output.FileOutputFormat;
import org.apache.hadoop.mapreduce.Counter;
import org.apache.hadoop.mapreduce.Counters;
import org.apache.hadoop.mapreduce.Job;
import org.apache.hadoop.mapreduce.Mapper;
public class MyCounter {
        public static enum MONTH{
                DEC,
                JAN,
                FEB
        };
public static class MyMapper extends Mapper<LongWritable, Text,
Text, Text> {
private Text out = new Text();
protected void map(LongWritable key, Text value, Context context)
throws java.io.IOException, InterruptedException {
        String line = value.toString();
        String[] strts = line.split(",");
        long lts = Long.parseLong(strts[1]);
        //The next two statements determines the month to which the
        log entry belongs
        Date time = new Date(lts);
        int m = time.getMonth();
        //Months are numbered from 0 to 11
        if(m==11){
                context.getCounter(MONTH.DEC).
                increment(10);
        }
        if(m==0){
                context.getCounter(MONTH.JAN).increment(20);
```

```
        }
        if(m==1){
                context.getCounter(MONTH.FEB).increment(30);
        }
                out.set("success");
         context.write(out,out);
        }
    }
    public static void main(String[] args) throws IOException,
    ClassNotFoundException, InterruptedException {
        Job job = new Job();
        job.setJarByClass(MyCounter.class);
        job.setJobName("CounterTest");
        job.setNumReduceTasks(0);
        job.setMapperClass(MyMapper.class);
        job.setMapOutputKeyClass(Text.class);
        job.setMapOutputValueClass(Text.class);
        FileInputFormat.addInputPath(job, new Path(args[0]));
        FileOutputFormat.setOutputPath(job, new Path(args[1]));
        job.waitForCompletion(true);
    //Gets the counter values and print the same to the console
        Counters counters = job.getCounters();
        Counter c1 = counters.findCounter(MONTH.DEC);
        System.out.println(c1.getDisplayName()+ ": " +
        c1.getValue());
        c1 = counters.findCounter(MONTH.JAN);
        System.out.println(c1.getDisplayName()+ ": " +
        c1.getValue());
        c1 = counters.findCounter(MONTH.FEB);
        System.out.println(c1.getDisplayName()+ ": " +
        c1.getValue());
    }
}
```

MRUNIT TESTING FRAMEWORK FOR TESTING MAPREDUCE CODE

Before starting, you need to download apache-mrunit-1.0.0-hadoop1. This contains the API for MRUnit testing framework. To set up the testing framework, you need to follow the steps provided below –

1. Open the eclipse project and import all the jars available in the lib folder of the downloaded file.
2. On the JRE system library, right click and configure build path by adding all the jars added for MRUnit testing framework.

In order to test mappers, you need to do the following –

1. Create an instance of the MapDriver class.
2. Next, an instance of the mapper must be added in the withMapper call.
3. The withInput call must pass the key and value that you need to give as inputs.
4. The withOutput call must be used for specifying the expected output.
5. The final call, runTest uses the input given using withInput and compares the output with the expected output given in the withOutput call.

Please note that MRUnit testing framework allows testing of only one input and output at a time. A sample implementation to learn how to use the testing framework is given below. This program tests a simple mapper that takes an input line. The mapper splits the input line on the basis of comma delimiter and uses the second word as key and 1 as value.

```
import java.io.IOException;
import junit.framework.TestCase;
import org.apache.hadoop.io.IntWritable;
import org.apache.hadoop.io.LongWritable;
import org.apache.hadoop.io.Text;
import org.apache.hadoop.mapreduce.Mapper;
```

```
import org.apache.hadoop.mrunit.mapreduce.*;
import org.junit.Test;

//The name of the file must be same as the name of the class
public class TestExample extends TestCase {
public static class maptest extends Mapper<LongWritable, Text, Text,
IntWritable>{
                Text day=new Text();
                public void map(LongWritable key, Text
                value,Context ct)
                throws IOException,InterruptedException {
                String[] line=value.toString().split(",");
                int val=Integer.parseInt(line[0]);
                day.set(line[1]);
                ct.write(day,new IntWritable(val));
                        }
                }
        /*We are using MapDriver because we are testing mapper
        here. This can be changed according to requirement*/
                MapDriver<LongWritable, Text, Text, IntWritable>
                mapDriver;
                public void setUp() {
                new maptest();
                mapDriver = MapDriver.newMapDriver( new
                maptest());
                }
                public void testMapper() {
                try {
                //The input line is 1,sunday,abhay,holiday
                //Running this test shall output (sunday, 1)
                        mapDriver.withInput(new LongWritable(),
new Text("1,sunday,abhay,holiday")).withOutput(new
Text("sunday"), new IntWritable(1)).runTest();
                        } catch (IOException e) {
```

```
                        e.printStackTrace();
                        }
                }
}
```

This test should return success. However, if you change the "1" value to "First Day" or change "sunday" to "Sunday", the test will fail. In a similar manner, other drivers can also be used for testing different phases of the MapReduce code.

EXERCISES

1. Implement the examples illustrated for –

    a. Combiner and Partitioner
    b. Map Side Join
    c. Reduce Side Join
    d. Counter

2. Implement the test case illustrated as example using the MRUnit framework.

Chapter 15

PIG COMMANDS AND SCRIPTING

INSTALL PIG

In order to install Apache Pig on Ubuntu, you can follow these steps –

Step 1:

You need to download the Pig file in your home directory by using cd. Go to the home directory and then run the following command –

wget http://www-us.apache.org/dist/pig/pig-0.16.0/pig-0.16.0.tar.gz

Step 2:

Untar the compressed file using the following command –

tar -xzf pig-0.16.0.tar.gz

Once you have run these two commands, do ls to check if this folder exists in your home directory.

Step 3:

Before you can use Pig, you need to set the environment variables by editing .bashrc file. You need to open the file in editing mode using the command:

gedit .bashrc

At the end of the file, just add these lines:

 # Set PIG Environment Variables
export PIG_HOME=$HOME/pig-0.16.0
export PATH=$PATH:$HOME/pig-0.16.0/bin
export PIG_CLASSPATH=$HADOOP_CONF_DIR

Step 4:

Update .bashrc by giving the command:

source .bashrc

Step 5:

To check if pig is running, run the following commands:

pig –version
pig –help

Both these commands must return valid results.

ENTER THE PIG GRUNT IN HDFS MODE

pig

ENTER THE PIG GRUNT IN LOCAL MODE

pig –x local

LOADING DATA FILES INTO THE PIG

grunt> <parameter> = LOAD '<filename with path>' using PigStorage(',');

Example:

In local mode:

grunt> a = LOAD 'A.txt' using PigStorage(',');

Here, A.txt is any file stored in the present working directory.

In HDFS mode:

> *grunt> a = LOAD 'hdfs:/A.txt' using PigStorage(',');*

Here, A.txt is any file stored in hdfs:/ directory.

EXPLICITLY DEFINING THE SCHEMA

> *grunt> <parameter> = LOAD '<filename with path>' using PigStorage(',') as <schema>;*

Example:

> *grunt> a = LOAD 'A.txt' using PigStorage(',') as (a:int, b:int, c:int);*

Here, 'a' is any variable. You can use the variable name of your choice.

PRINTING THE CONTENTS OF A PARAMETER ON THE CONSOLE.

> *grunt> dump <parameter>;*

Example:

> *grunt> dump a;*

OPERATING ON LOADED DATA

> *grunt> a = LOAD 'A.txt' using PigStorage(',');*
> *grunt> b = LOAD 'B.txt' using PigStorage(',');*
> *grunt> c = UNION a, b;*
> *grunt> dump c;*

Here, A.txt and B.txt are sample files. The contents of the two files are follows:

A.txt	B.txt
0,1,2	0,5,2
1,3,4	1,7,8

Please note that no caching is performed. Data is read directly from the HDFS and relation definitions are stored in the memory.

APPLYING CONDITIONAL OPERATORS ON DATA OPERATIONS

grunt> SPLIT c INTO d IF $0==0, e IF $0==1;
grunt> dump d;
grunt> dump e;

This commands splits the c data into two sub-datasets – d and e. If the value of the first column element ($0) is 0, the row is assigned to d. However, if the value of the first column element ($0) is 1, the row is assigned to e.

WORD COUNT EXAMPLE IN PIG

Steps for running the word count example are provided below.

1. Create a sample file using gedit
   gedit wc_sample.txt
2. Copy the file to HDFS
   hadoop fs –put wc_sample.txt <path in hdfs>
3. Enter Pig grunt
   pig
4. Load the data file into the Pig grunt
   grunt> A = LOAD 'wc_sample.txt' using PigStorage(',');
   grunt> B = FOREACH A GENERATE FLATTEN(TOKENIZE((chararray)$0)) as word;
   grunt> C = GROUP B by word;
   grunt> D = FOREACH C GENERATE group, COUNT(B);
   grunt> dump D;

CREATING PIG SCRIPTS

- Copy the following commands for word count example into a text file and name it wc_example.pig
  grunt> A = LOAD 'wc_sample.txt' using PigStorage(',');
  grunt> B = FOREACH A GENERATE
  FLATTEN(TOKENIZE((chararray)$0)) as word;

grunt> C = GROUP B by word;
grunt> D = FOREACH C GENERATE group, COUNT(B);

- Add the following command to the end of the file to store the output into a directory.
  STORE D INTO 'hdfs:/output_wc';
- Save the file and run the following command on the command line:
  pig wc_example.pig
- Check the logs and output directory to see the output

USER DEFINED FUNCTIONS (UDF)

The set of steps given below creates a UDF called myUpper that converts all the lower case characters in the sample text file to upper case characters.

1. Create a java file using Eclipse (just like it is done for MapReduce programs).
2. Create a jar file corresponding to the created java file.
   Do not forget to include library files for Pig in the Build Path. There are three files that are usually found in usr/lib/pig directory. Also, ensure that classname is same as filename.
3. Create input file using gedit. Name the file x.txt with the following contents.

```
This is a sample file.
```

4. Create a Pig script for converting all lower case characters to upper case characters. Name the file demo.pig and put the following contents into it.

```
register /<absolute_path>/demo.jar;
A = LOAD '/<path>/x.txt' USING PigStorage('\t') as
(Fname:chararray; Lname:chararray; MobileNo:chararray);
B = FOREACH A GENERATE myUpper($0);
STORE B INTO '/<path>/op_dir';
DUMP B;
```

5. Move the sample text file x.txt to HDFS from local using copyFromLocal.
6. Run the Pig script using the following command –

   pig demo.pig

7. Check the output.

EXITING THE PIG GRUNT

grunt> quit;

EXERCISE

Using weather data of a year for a city, determine the following:

a. Find hot days (days when temperature > 25).
b. Find cold days (days when temperature < 0).
c. Find the hottest day of the year.
d. Find the coldest day of the year.

You can create a dummy dataset to test the solution.

Chapter 16

HIVE COMMANDS AND SCRIPTING

INSTALL HIVE

To install Apache Hive on Ubuntu, you need to follow the steps given below.

Step 1:

You need to download the Hive tar file in the home directory. Firstly, go to the home directory using cd command and give the following command:

> *wget http://archive.apache.org/dist/hive/hive-2.1.0/apache-hive-2.1.0-bin.tar.gz*

Step 2:

Untar the file using the command given below.

> *tar -xzf apache-hive-2.1.0-bin.tar.gz*

Once these two commands have been executed, perform ls command to check if the folder has been created in your home directory.

Step 3:

Set the environment variables for Hive by editing.bashrc file. To open the file in editing mode, give the command:

gedit .bashrc

At the end of the file, add these lines:

 # Set HIVE environment variables
export HIVE_HOME=$HOME/apache-hive-2.1.0-bin
export PATH=$PATH:$HOME/apache-hive-2.1.0-bin/bin

Step 4:

To implement the changes made to .bashrc file, give the command:

source .bashrc

Step 5:

Now that you have reached so far, check the Hive version to see if all is as expected by running the following command:

hive --version

Step 6:

Now, you need to create directory in HDFS where Hive can store its created tables. For this, you need to give the following set of commands.

hdfs dfs -mkdir -p /user/hive/warehouse
hdfs dfs -mkdir /tmp

Step 7:

The group needs to have read/write permissions for the folders. The following commands are used to change the mode.

hdfs dfs -chmod g+w /user/hive/warehouse
hdfs dfs -chmod g+w /tmp

Step 8:

The Hadoop path needs to be set in hive.env.sh. For this, you need to open the file in editing mode using these commands:

```
cd apache-hive-2.1.0-bin/
gedit conf/hive-env.sh
```

Add these lines:

```
#Set HADOOP_HOME
export HADOOP_HOME=$HOME/hadoop-2.7.3
export HADOOP_HEAPSIZE=512
#Set HIVE_CONF_DIR
export HIVE_CONF_DIR=$HOME/apache-hive-2.1.0-bin/conf
```

Step 9:

Make the below stated changes to hive-site.xml. For this, you need to open the file in editing mode using the following command:

```
gedit conf/hive-site.xml
```

Now change the configuration by adding properties according to the text given below:

```
<configuration>
<property>
<name>javax.jdo.option.ConnectionURL</name>
<value>jdbc:derby:;databaseName=/home/edureka/apache-hive-
2.1.0-bin/metastore_db;create=true</value>
<description>
JDBC connect string for a JDBC metastore.
To use SSL to encrypt/authenticate the connection, provide database-
specific SSL flag in the connection URL.
For example, jdbc:postgresql://myhost/db?ssl=true for postgres database.
</description>
</property>
<property>
<name>hive.metastore.warehouse.dir</name>
<value>/user/hive/warehouse</value>
```

```
<description>location of default database for the warehouse</
description>
</property>
<property>
<name>hive.metastore.uris</name>
<value/>
<description>Thrift URI for the remote metastore. Used by metastore
client to connect to remote metastore.</description>
</property>
<property>
<name>javax.jdo.option.ConnectionDriverName</name>
<value>org.apache.derby.jdbc.EmbeddedDriver</value>
<description>Driver class name for a JDBC metastore</description>
</property>
<property>
<name>javax.jdo.PersistenceManagerFactoryClass</name>
<value>org.datanucleus.api.jdo.JDOPersistenceManagerFactory</
value>
<description>class implementing the jdo persistence</description>
</property>
</configuration>
```

Step 10:

Hive uses Derby database, by default. Therefore, before starting work in Hive, you need to initialize Derby database using the following command:

```
bin/schematool -initSchema -dbType derby
```

Once you are through with these commands, you are all set to launch hive.

TO START HIVE AND ENTER THE HIVE SHELL

```
hive
```

SHOWING ALL TABLES IN THE WORKING HIVE DATABASE

```
hive> show tables;
```

CREATING A DATABASE

```
hive> create database <db_name>;
```

Example:

```
hive> create database db_emp;
```

SPECIFYING WORKING DATABASE AND CREATE TABLES INSIDE THAT DATABASE

```
hive> use <db_name>;
```

Example:

```
hive> use db_emp;
```

CREATING A TABLE

Two types of tables can be created in Hive namely, managed tables and external tables. Managed tables are tables created in HDFS for which data needs to be loaded separately. On the other hand, external tables link the table to an external file with the data.

(a) Managed Table

```
hive> create table <table_name>(
    >comma separated schema
    >)
    >row format delimited fields terminated by ‘,’;
```

Example:

```
hive> create table tb_emp(
    >model string,
    >id int,
    >brand string
    >)
    >row format delimited fields terminated by ‘,’;
```

(b) External Tables

```
hive> create external table <table_name>(
    >comma separated schema
    >)
    >row format delimited fields terminated by ','
    >LOCATION '<path>';
```

Example:

```
hive> create external table tb_emp_ext(
    >model string,
    >id int,
    >brand string
    >)
    >row format delimited fields terminated by ','
    >LOCATION 'hdfs:/';
```

Please note that data is linked to the table while creating the table in case of external tables. Therefore, if you have the data file in local filesystem, you will need to copy the file from the local filesystem to HDFS using copyFromLocal or put. On the other hand, data needs to be loaded after table creation for managed tables.

ADDING DATA TO MANAGED HIVE TABLES

```
hive> LOAD DATA LOCAL INPATH '<local path>' INTO TABLE tb_emp;
```

RUNNING QUERIES

```
hive> select * from tb_emp;
```

LOCATION OF DATABASE FOLDER, TABLE FOLDERS AND DATA FILES:

```
$ hadoop fs –ls /user/hive/warehouse/
```

DELETING A TABLE

```
hive> drop table tb_emp;
```

DELETING A DATABASE

hive> drop database db_emp;

Please note that all the tables created inside a database must be deleted before deleting the database.

TO QUIT HIVE

hive> quit;

MANAGING OUTPUTS

The output of a Hive query can be redirected to another table, a local file or HDFS, on requirement basis. The commands to enforce the same have been given below.

- Inserting output into a local file

  *INSERT OVERWRITE LOCAL DIRECTORY 'query_result' SELECT * FROM sample_table;*

- Inserting output into HDFS

  *INSERT OVERWRITE DIRECTORY 'query_result' SELECT * FROM sample_table;*

- Inserting output into a table

  *INSERT OVERWRITE TABLE query_result(SELECT * FROM sample_table);*

HIVE SCRIPTS

Scripts in Hive are created in the same manner as in Pig. However, Hive scripts are named with the extension .hql (Example – sample.hql). To run a script, the following command needs to be given from the command line (not the Hive shell).

$ hive –f sample.hql

EQUIJOIN IN HIVE

To perform a join, create two sample files for which the join needs to be performed. Then, create tables for the datasets that need to be joined. For example, we wish to join two tables, one of which is the employee data table and the other contains the email ids of the employees. Name of the employee is the common column between the two tables. Hive statements for performing this operation is given below.

```
hive> CREATE TABLE emp_table(name STRING, salary FLOAT, city STRING)
    > row format delimited fields terminated by ',';
hive> CREATE TABLE emailid(name STRING, email STRING)
    > row format delimited fields terminated by ',';
hive> LOAD DATA LOCAL INPATH 'sampleemp.txt' INTO TABLE emp_table;
hive> LOAD DATA LOCAL INPATH 'emailids.txt' INTO TABLE emailid;
```

Please note that you need to give absolute paths of the sample text files for the system to find them. Before moving forward, check if the data has been loaded into the tables.

```
hive> SELECT * FROM emp_table;
hive> SELECT * FROM emailid;
```

To perform inner join on two tables, you can use the following SQL statement.

```
hive> SELECT a.name, a.salary, a.city FROM emp_table a JOIN emailid ON a.name=b.name;
```

To perform left outer join on two tables, you can use the following SQL statement.

```
hive> SELECT a.name, a.salary, a.city FROM emp_table a LEFT OUTER JOIN emailid ON a.name=b.name;
```

To perform right outer join on two tables, you can use the following SQL statement.

hive> SELECT a.name, a.salary, a.city FROM emp_table a RIGHT OUTER JOIN emailid ON a.name=b.name;

CREATING PARTITIONS AND BUCKETS IN HIVE

Partitioning and bucketing can be performed dynamically or statically. We will discuss both these cases in this section.

Dynamic Partitioning and Bucketing

In order to create partitions and buckets, you need to mention the database in use, create a table and define the partition and bucketing scheme for the table. Sample code for this is given below.

```
hive>use dbtxn;
hive>CREATE TABLE txnrecords(txnnum INT, txndate STRING, custid INT, txnamount DOUBLE, txnproduct STRING, txnstate STRING)
> PARTITIONED BY (txncategory STRING)
> CLUSTERED BY (txnstate) INTO 5 buckets
> row format delimited fields terminated by ',';
```

The commands given above create a table in the database and define the partitioning and bucketing scheme for the table. However, if you run the following query, no records will appear as result.

```
hive>SELECT * FROM txnrecords LIMIT 10;
```

The reason for this is that we have not added any records to the table. Now, if we add records to the table, they must be dynamically partitioned. For this, a few parameters need to be set using the given set of commands.

```
$ set hive.exec.dynamic.partition.mode=nonstrict;
$ set hive.exec.dynamic.partition=true;
$ set hive.enforce.bucketing=true;
```

Now, insert data from an existing table txntable to this table using the following command:

```
hive>FROM txntable txn INSERT OVERWRITE TABLE txnrecords PARTITION(txncategory)
> SELECT txnnum, txndate, custid, txnamount, txnproduct, txnstate, txncategory DISTRIBUTE BY txncategory;
```

You can look at the folders and files created for every partition and bucket by listing the contents of the datawarehouse directory inside Hive (as stated above).

Static Partitioning and Bucketing

Partitions can be statically added to tables. Let us look at an example to see how static partitions can be created in Hive.

```
hive> CREATE TABLE sample table(
> name STRING,
> id INT)
> PARTITIONED BY (year INT)
> row format delimited fields terminated by '\t';
```

Since there is no data in the table, no partitions have been created. To add a partition, the following command needs to be given.

```
hive> ALTER TABLE sample table ADD PARTITION(year=2017);
```

You can delete the partition using drop command as well. To add data, create a sample file (tab separated data), named sam.txt.

```
$hadoop fs -put sam.txt /user/hive/warehouse/dbtxn.db/sampletable/
year=2017/
```

Now, if you query the table for records, you will see the records along with their date of creation.

CUSTOM MAPREDUCE SCRIPTS AND UDF

Programmers can extend the capabilities of Hive by plugging in traditional MapReduce scripts for sophisticated data analysis. This feature has been added, to Hive, to give programmers the flexibility to integrate their code to the Hive shell and gain maximum performance-ease of use tradeoff from this tool. In order to understand how custom MapReduce code can be integrated with Hive, let us take an example.

1. Create table (say sample_table)
2. Insert data into the table
3. Create python script for desired functionality. The code must be written in such a manner that each record is read, modified and the required value is returned.
4. Add the python or java file using the following command.
   hive> ADD FILE '<complete path of python or java code for the required functionality>'
   Example:
   hive> ADD FILE 'sample_map_code.py'
5. Create a new table for saving the transformed results (say *new_table*)
6. Use INSERT command to add result as shown below.
   hive> INSERT OVERWRITE TABLE new_table
   SELECT
   TRANSFORM (x_field, y_field, z_field)
   AS (x_field, mod_y_field, z_field)
   FROM sample_data;
   In this example, a column of the sample_table (y_field) is being transformed into mod_y_field using the custom mapper code written in Java or Python and the result of the transformation is saved in another table named new_table.

To create a UDF, you need to create a jar file for the desired functionality's logic by creating a class that extends the class UDF. The steps involved in creating a UDF are as follows –

1. Create table (say sample_table)
2. Load data into the table
3. Create JAR file for desired functionality.
4. Add the JAR file using the command:

   hive> ADD JAR '<complete path of python or java code for the required functionality>'

   Example:

   hive> ADD JAR 'sample_jar.jar'
5. Create a temporary function that uses the class created in the JAR using the command:

   hive> CREATE TEMPORARY FUNCTION samplefunc AS 'Sample_Class';
6. Apply the temporary function on the column using the command:

   hive> SELECT samp_col(samplefunc) FROM sample_table

The output shall print out the transformed result on the screen.

EXERCISE

Using database of movies with movie name, movie release date and movie rating, find the following:

1. List all the movies with rating < 5 and rating > 3
2. List all movies released before year = 2000
3. Sort movies on the basis of release date (most recent movie first)
4. Find average rating of all movies released in the year 1998

You can use a dummy dataset to test the solution.

Chapter 17

WORKING IN HBASE

INSTALL HBASE

In order to install HBase on Ubuntu, you need to follow the steps given below.

Step 1:

Firstly, you need to download the HBase tar file in your home directory. For that, enter your home directory using cd command. Then, give the following command:

wget http://mirror.tcpdiag.net/apache/hbase/hbase-0.90.6/hbase-0.90.6.tar.gz

Step 2:

Extract the file contents using the command:

tar -xzf hbase-0.90.6.tar.gz

Step 3:

HBase storage requires a dedicated folder, which needs to be created using the command:

mkdir hbaseStorage

Step 4:

You need to edit the hbase-site.xml file. For this, you need to first change your directory using the command:

```
cd hbase-0.90.6/
```

Then, open the file in editing mode using the command:

```
gedit conf/hbase-site.xml
```

Change the contents of the file to:

```
<?xml version=”1.0”?>
<?xml-stylesheet type=”text/xsl” href=”configuration.xsl”?>
<configuration>
<property>
<name>hbase.rootdir</name> <value>file:///home/ubuntu/
hbaseStorage/hbase</value>
</property> <property>
<name>hbase.zookeeper.property.dataDir</name>
<value>/hbaseStorage/zookeeper</value> </property>
</configuration>
```

Now, you are all set to start working with HBase.

GETTING STARTED

To start HBase, you need to go to the HBase folder and type the following command:

```
./bin/start-hbase.sh
```

To enter the HBase shell, use the command –

```
hbase shell
```

LIST EXISTING TABLE

To list tables already present in HBase, type the following command:

list

CREATE TABLE

In order to create tables in HBase, the following command needs to be used.

create 'table_name', 'column_family'

Example:

create 's_table', 'studentdetails'

VIEW TABLE DETAILS

In order to view details of the table created in HBase, the command is:

describe 'table_name'

Example:

describe 's_table'

INSERT DATA

To insert data in a table, type the command:

put 'hbase_table_name', 'rowkey', 'column_family_name:column_name', 'value'

Example:

put 's_table', 'student1', 'studentdetails:name, 'abc'
put 's_table', 'student1', 'studentdetails:course, 'mca'
put 's_table', 'student1', 'studentdetails:gender', 'male'
put 's_table', 'student2', 'studentdetails:name, 'xyz
put 's_table', 'student2', 'studentdetails:course, 'bca'
put 's_table', 'student2', 'studentdetails:gender', 'male'

UPDATE DATA

To update data in a table, type the command:

put 'hbase_table_name', 'rowkey', 'column_family:column_name', 'value_update'

Example:

put 's_table, 'student1', 'studentdetails:gender', 'female'

SELECT DATA/QUERY TABLE

If you wish to see all the contents of the table, you can use the command:

scan 'table_name'

However, if you wish to retrieve a particular record from the table, then you need to use the following command and give the rowkey corresponding to the record required.

get 'table_name', 'rowkey'

The get command can be broken down to column level for retrieving the smallest entity of data.

get 'table_name', 'rowkey', 'column_family:column_name'

Example:

scan 's_table'
get 's_table', 'student2', 'studentdetails:gender'

If you don't know the rowkey, you can do a full scan, see the rowkey and then give the required command.

DELETE DATA

To delete records, the following command can be used.

delete 'table_name', 'rowkey', 'column_family:column_name'

Example:

delete 's_table', 'student1', 'studentdetails:gender'

Once you run this command, you will see that a scan will show only 2 records for student2.

ALTER TABLE

Before altering a table, you need to disable the table using the following command. Once the table is disabled, it can be altered. To make the table usable again, it needs to be enabled.

disable 'table_name'
alter 'table_name', {NAME=> 'column_family'}
enable 'table_name'

Example:

disable 's_table'
alter 's_table', {NAME=> 'fellowshipdetails'}
enable 's_table'

You can use describe command to see how the column family details for the table have changed. Once the column family has been added, you can add records to this column family. For example –

put 's_table', 'student2', 'fellowshipdetails:organization, 'comp'

A scan will now show 3 records for student2: 2 corresponding to studentdetails and 1 corresponding to fellowshipdetails.

DROP TABLE

To drop a table, the following command needs to be executed.

disable 'table_name'
drop 'table_name'

Example:

disable 's_table'
drop 's_table'

EXERCISE

Create a table for storing employee data and perform all the operations listed above.

Chapter 18

JOB MANAGEMENT IN OOZIE

INSTALLING OOZIE

In order to install Oozie on a single node cluster, you need to follow the steps given below.

Step 1:

Firstly, you need to download the tar file into your home directory using the following command –

$ wget http://supergsego.com/apache/oozie/3.3.2/oozie-3.3.2.tar.gz

Step 2:

Now, untar the downloaded file using the command:

$ tar xvzf oozie-3.3.2.tar.gz

Step 3:

Build Oozie using the following set of commands –

$ cd oozie-3.3.2/bin
$ ./mkdistro.sh –DskipTests

Step 4:

In order to setup the Oozie server, you need to execute the commands given below –

```
$ cd ../../
$ cp -R oozie-3.3.2/distro/target/oozie-3.3.2-distro/oozie-3.3.2/ oozie
```

Step 5:

Oozie server requires a libtext directory, which needs to be created using the following commands –

```
$ cd oozie
$ mkdir libext
$ cp ../oozie-3.3.2/hadooplibs/target/oozie-3.3.2-hadooplibs.tar.gz .
$ tar xzvf oozie-3.3.2-hadooplibs.tar.gz
$ cp oozie-3.3.2/hadooplibs/hadooplib-1.1.1.oozie-3.3.2/* libext/
```

In order to support the web console facility, Ext2Js library is required. This needs to be downloaded separately and included in the libtext folder.

```
$ cd libext
$ wget http://extjs.com/deploy/ext-2.2.zip
$ cd ..
```

Step 6:

Make the required changes in ../hadoop/conf/core-site.xml file by opening it using gedit and adding the following properties to the configuration file –

```
<property>
<name>hadoop.proxyuser.hduser.hosts</name>
<value>localhost</value>
</property>
<property>
<name>hadoop.proxyuser.hduser.groups</name>
```

<value>hadoop</value>
</property>

Here, 'hduser' is the username and it belongs to 'hadoop' group.

Step 7:

Lastly, you need to prepare the WAR file.

$ ./bin/oozie-setup.sh prepare-war

After the successful execution of this command, Oozie shall be ready to start.

Step 8:

In order to create sharelib on HDFS, the following command needs to be executed –

$ ./bin/oozie-setup.sh sharelib create -fs hdfs://localhost:54310

Please note that the destination path for sharelib is: /user/hduser/share/lib

Step 9:

The next step creates OoozieDB. For this, the command is –

$ ./bin/ooziedb.sh create -sqlfile oozie.sql -run

Step 10:

Check the status of Oozie.

To start Oozie as a daemon, use the command:

$ ./bin/oozied.sh start

To start Oozie as a foreground process use the command:

$ ./bin/oozied.sh run

You can also check the log file to see if Oozie started normally. The log file is available at: *logs/oozie.log*. Besides this, the status of Oozie can be checked using -

$ ./bin/oozie admin -oozie http://localhost:11000/oozie -status

It should show NORMAL if all is good.

The web console can be accessed at –

http://localhost:11000/oozie

Step 11:

In order to set up the client for Oozie, the following commands need to be executed –

$ cd ..
$ cp oozie/oozie-client-3.3.2.tar.gz .
$ tar xvzf oozie-client-3.3.2.tar.gz
$ mv oozie-client-3.3.2 oozie-client
$ cd bin

Step 12:

Finally, add the Oozie path '$HOME/oozie-client/bin' to .bashrc file and restart the terminal. The Oozie Server and Client setup on a single node cluster is now ready. To start Oozie, go in the Oozie folder and give the following command –

./bin/oozie-start.sh

RUNNING A JOB IN OOZIE

In order to run an application with Oozie, you need to follow the steps given below. However, you need to understand that running an application is a two-step process. You first create the application and then, run it. Therefore, the first few steps involve application creation while the last step illustrates how to run the application.

Step 1:

Create a directory for the job

Step 2:

Create the jar file for the job and copy it to a sub-folder named lib in the job directory.

Step 3:

Inside the job directory, create job.properties and workflow.xml.

Step 4:

Move this directory to the HDFS

Step 5:

Run the application using the command:

> *$oozie job –oozie http://localhost:11000/oozie -config job.properties --run*

Remember that the file job.properties is saved locally and it is provided here from its local path.

MONITORING A JOB

The status of a workflow job can be viewed by giving the command:

> *$oozie job –info <job-id>*

The workflow job log can be accessed using the command:

> *$oozie job –log <job-id>*

Job definition can be found using the command:

> *$oozie job –definition <job-id>*

It is important to mention that job-id can be seen from the web interface.

OTHER OOZIE COMMANDS

To check the status of multiple workflow jobs, the following command can be given -

$oozie jobs -oozie http://localhost:11000/oozie -localtime -len 2 -filter status=RUNNING

To check the status of multiple coordinator jobs, the command (given below) can be given -

$oozie jobs -oozie http://localhost:11000/oozie -jobtype coordinator

If you wish to kill a job (workflow, coordinator or bundle job), give the command mentioned below -

$oozie jobs -oozie http://localhost:11000/oozie -kill 14-20090525161321-oozie-joe

On the contrary, you may also check the status of a job (workflow, coordinator or bundle job) using the command:

$oozie jobs -oozie http://localhost:11000/oozie -info 14-20090525161321-oozie-joe

You can also check the version of Oozie running on the system by giving the command:

$oozie admin -oozie http://localhost/oozie -version

EXERCISE

Let us take the wordcount file and run the wordcount example as an Oozie job. For this, you need to follow the given steps and implement them in accordance with the steps mentioned for job execution (as mentioned above).

Step 1:

Create workflow.xml.

```
<workflow-app nome='wordcount –wf'>
<start to= 'wordcount'/>
<action name='Wordcount'>
<map-reduce>
<job-tracker>foo.com:9001</job-tracker>
<name-node>hdfs://bar.com:9000</name-node>
<configuration>
<property>
<name>mapred.input.dir</name>
<value>${inputDir}</value,>
</property>
<property>
<name>mapred.output.dir</name>
<value> ${outputDir}</value>
</property>
</configuration>
</map-reduce>
<ok to='end'/>
<error to='kill'/>
</action>
<kill name='kill'/>
<end name='end'/>
</Workflow-app>
```

Step 2:

Deploy the application.

```
$ hadoop fs-put wordcount-wf hdfs://bar.com:9000/usr/abc/
wordcount
```

Step 3:

Set the workflow job parameters.

```
$ cat job.properites
Oozie.wf.application.path=hdfs://bar.com:9000/usr/abc/wordcount
Input=/usr/abc/input-data
Output=/usr/abc/output-data
```

Step 4:

```
$ oozie job –run –config job.properties
```

Chapter 19

DATA LOADING TECHNIQUES

It will not be possible to implement a complete Hadoop/Big Data project until data can be imported from different sources into the HDFS. There are three data loading techniques available, which are as follows –

1. Sqoop – used for import of structured data
2. Flume – used for import of unstructured and semi-structured data
3. Hadoop Commands (get or CopyFromLocal and put or CopyToLocal) – used for import of data from the local filesystem.

Another command used for data loading is distcp. It is a command, which is used to move data between clusters for purposes of taking backup or recovery. The syntax of this command is –

$hadoop distcp hdfs://<source> hdfs://<target>

SQOOP

Installing Sqoop

In order to install Sqoop, the following steps need to be followed. However, please note that Java and Hadoop must be already installed on the system. Check their versions to verify that these prerequisites are installed on the system before you start with Sqoop installation.

Step 1:

Download the Sqoop tar in the home directory using the command:

$wget sqoop-1.4.5.bin__hadoop-2.0.4-alpha.tar.gz

Step 2:

Untar the file using the command:

$tar -xvf sqoop-1.4.4.bin__hadoop-2.0.4-alpha.tar.gz

Step 3:

Edit the .bashrc file by opening it using gedit and adding the following content to it.

```
#Sqoop
export SQOOP_HOME=$HOME/sqoop
export PATH=$PATH:$SQOOP_HOME/bin
```

In order to implement the changes made, run the command:

$source ~/.bashrc

Step 4:

Now that you have set the *SQOOP_HOME* variable, you need to set environment variables to the sqoop-env.sh file, which is placed in the *$SQOOP_HOME/conf* directory. The following set of commands needs to be run for this purpose.

```
$ cd $SQOOP_HOME/conf
$ mv sqoop-env-template.sh sqoop-env.sh
```

Now, open the sqoop-env.sh file using gedit and add the following lines to it.

```
export HADOOP_MAPRED_HOME=$HOME/hadoop-2.7.3
export HADOOP_COMMON_HOME=$HOME/hadoop-2.7.3
```

Step 5:

The next step involves the downloading and configuration of the mysql-connector. The tar file for the mysql-connector can be downloaded into the home directory from the following link –

http://ftp.ntu.edu.tw/MySQL/Downloads/Connector-J/

Once you have downloaded the tar file, you need to untar it using the following command –

```
$tar -zxf mysql-connector-java-5.1.30.tar.gz
```

The configuration part requires you to run the following commands –

```
$cd mysql-connector-java-5.1.30
$mv mysql-connector-java-5.1.30-bin.jar /usr/lib/sqoop/lib
```

Step 6:

Lastly, check the Sqoop version to verify if the installation has been successfully completed.

```
$cd $SQOOP_HOME/bin
$sqoop-version
```

Importing Data from Table

The general syntax for running a Sqoop import is as follows –

```
$sqoop import (generic-args) (import-args)
$sqoop-import (generic-args) (import-args)
```

Example –

Assuming that the database in MySQL database server is named userdb. In order to import a table named employee, you need to run the following command –

```
$sqoop import \
--connect jdbc:mysql://localhost/userdb \
```

```
--username root \
--table employee --m 1
```

You can check if the table has been imported by accessing the file located in the following directory –

```
HADOOP_HOME/bin/hadoop fs -cat /employee
```

If you open the part files, you will see that the data is comma-separated.

Importing Data from Table into Target Directory

If you wish to import the table into a target directory, you will need to add the following flag to the import command –

```
--target-dir <new or exist directory in HDFS>
```

Example –

Assuming that there is another table named employee_1. To import this table into a target directory named t_dir, you need to give the following command –

```
$sqoop import \
--connect jdbc:mysql://localhost/userdb \
--username root \
--table employee_1 \
--m 1 \
--target-dir /t_dir
```

You can verify the import by running the command:

```
$HADOOP_HOME/bin/hadoop fs -cat /t_dir/part-m-*
```

Importing Subset of Data from Table

You can use the WHERE clause to import only a subset of the table. The example given below will show you how this can be done.

```
$sqoop import \
--connect jdbc:mysql://localhost/userdb \
```

```
--username root \
--table employee_1 \
--m 1 \
--where "city ='delhi'" \
--target-dir /t_dir_delhi
```

In order to verify if the import has been successfully made, you can run the following command –

```
$HADOOP_HOME/bin/hadoop fs -cat /t_dir_delhi/part-m-*
```

Incremental Import

This functionality allows you to add only the rows that have been newly added to the table. The syntax for the same is –

```
--incremental <mode>
--check-column <column name>
--last value <last check column value>
```

Example –

```
$sqoop import \
--connect jdbc:mysql://localhost/userdb \
--username root \
--table employee \
--m 1 \
--incremental append \
--check-column id \
-last value 1199
```

This command will check if the column ID value of 1200 and onwards exists. If yes, the rows will be imported and the table employee will be accordingly appended.

Importing All Tables

All the tables of the database can be imported using the following command –

```
$ sqoop import-all-tables \
--connect jdbc:mysql://localhost/userdb \
--username root
```

Exporting Data

Please note that the table to be exported must be available in HDFS. Assuming that the file, employee_file is available in employee/ directory of HDFS. In order to export the table to MySQL, a corresponding table should be created in MySQL using the following command –

```
$mysql
mysql> USE usrdb;
mysql> CREATE TABLE employee_exp (
id INT NOT NULL PRIMARY KEY,
name VARCHAR(20),
salary INT,
address VARCHAR(10));
```

In order to export the table in HDFS to MySQL, you need to give the following command –

```
$sqoop export \
--connect jdbc:mysql://localhost/db \
--username root \
--table employee_exp \
--export-dir /employee/employee_file
```

You can check if the table has been successfully exported by running SELECT * query from the mysql prompt.

List Databases

The following command lists all the databases –

```
$ sqoop list-databases \
--connect jdbc:mysql://localhost/ \
--username root
```

List Tables

The following command lists all the tables in the userdb database –

```
$sqoop list-tables \
--connect jdbc:mysql://localhost/userdb \
--username root
```

Sqoop Jobs

Sqoop jobs can be created and managed for implementing functionalities like repetitive incremental imports. A Sqoop job can be created using the command:

```
$sqoop job (generic-args) (job-args)
[-- [subtool-name] (subtool-args)]
```

Example –

In order to create Sqoop job that imports a table employee_1 into database usrdb, you need to give the following set of commands.

```
$sqoop job --create job_1 \
--import \
--connect jdbc:mysql://localhost/usrdb \
--username root \
--table employee_1 --m 1
```

To verify if the job has been created, you can run the command that gives a list of Sqoop jobs, which is as follows –

```
$sqoop job --list
```

You can also inspect a specific job (job_1) using the command:

$sqoop job --show job_1

The job can be executed using the command:

$sqoop job --exec job_1

IMPORTING DATA USING FLUME

Installing Flume

To install Flume, you need to follow the steps mentioned below.

Step 1:

Firstly, visit the link –

https://flume.apache.org/

Download the latest version of Flume in the home directory named apache-flume-1.6.0-bin.tar.gz. Untar the downloaded file using the command:

$tar zxvf apache-flume-1.6.0-bin.tar.gz

Step 2:

In order to configure Flume, three files namely flume-env.sh, flumeconf.properties, and .bashrc need to be edited. Open the .bashrc file and add the content given below.

```
#Flume
export FLUME_HOME=$HOME/apache-flume-1.6.0-bin.tar
export PATH=$PATH:/FLUME_HOME/bin
export CLASSPATH=$CLASSPATH:/FLUME_HOME/lib/*
```

Now, enter the conf directory in the flume directory and rename the flume-conf.properties.template as flume –conf.properties and flume-env.sh.template as flume-env.sh. Now open flume-env.sh file using gedit and add the JAVA_HOME path by adding the below-mentioned line.

export JAVA_HOME=$HOME/jdk1.8.0_101

Step 3:

Once installed, you can verify the installation by running the command –

$./flume-ng

Configuring Import from Source

In order to configure import from a source, using Flume, the configuration file needs to be appropriately edited by adding the following –

- Naming the components of the current agent
- Configuring the source
- Configuring the channel
- Configuring the sink
- Binding the source and sink to the channel

The components are named by setting values to the parameters in the below-mentioned manner.

agent_name.sources = source_name
agent_name.sinks = sink_name
agent_name.channels = channel_name

The sources, channels and sinks supported by Flume include –

Sources	Channels	Sinks
Avro Source	Memory Channel	HDFS Sink
Thrift Source	JDBC Channel	Hive Sink
Exec Source	Kafka Channel	Logger Sink
JMS Source	File Channel	Avro Sink
Spooling Directory Source	Spillable Memory Channel	Thrift Sink
Twitter 1% firehose Source	Pseudo Transaction Channel	IRC Sink
Kafka Source		File Roll Sink
NetCat Source		Null Sink
Sequence Generator Source		HBaseSink

Sources	Channels	Sinks
Syslog Sources		AsyncHBaseSink
Syslog TCP Source		MorphlineSolrSink
Multiport Syslog TCP Source		ElasticSearchSink
Syslog UDP Source		Kite Dataset Sink
HTTP Source		Kafka Sink
Stress Source		
Legacy Sources		
Thrift Legacy Source		
Custom Source		
Scribe Source		

In order to configure the source, the following parameters must be set.

agent_name.sources. source_name.type = value
agent_name.sources. source_name.property2 = value
agent_name.sources. source_name.property3 = value

The sink also has a set of properties that need to be set in the following manner –

agent_name.sinks. sink_name.type = value
agent_name.sinks. sink_name.property2 = value
agent_name.sinks. sink_name.property3 = value

To connect the source to the sink, the channel needs to be described. For this, the following parameters must be set.

agent_name.channels.channel_name.type = value
agent_name.channels.channel_name. property2 = value
agent_name.channels.channel_name. property3 = value

Now that the channel has been described, it must be connected to the source and the sink by setting the following parameters.

agent_name.sources.source_name.channels = channel_name
agent_name.sinks.sink_name.channels = channel_name

Example – Fetching Data from Twitter

Fetching data from Twitter is a three-step process, which include –

- Creation of Twitter application
  To create a Twitter application, you need to visit the Twitter website and follow the link given below –
  https://apps.twitter.com/
  Create a new application and generate access tokens.
- Starting HDFS
  Start all the daemons of Hadoop and create a directory for data to be imported using the following commands –
  $cd /$Hadoop_Home/bin/
  $hdfs dfs -mkdir hdfs://localhost:9000/user/Hadoop/twitter_data
- Configuring Flume
  Firstly, the source, sink and channel need to be named and defined. Besides this, the source and sink need to bind to the channel. For this, the parameter values will be as follows –
  - Naming Components
    TwitterAgent.sources = Twitter
    TwitterAgent.channels = MemChannel
    TwitterAgent.sinks = HDFS
  - Defining Source
    TwitterAgent.sources.Twitter.type = org.apache.flume.source.twitter.TwitterSource
    TwitterAgent.sources.Twitter.consumerKey = Your OAuth consumer key
    TwitterAgent.sources.Twitter.consumerSecret = Your OAuth consumer secret
    TwitterAgent.sources.Twitter.accessToken = Your OAuth consumer key access token
    TwitterAgent.sources.Twitter.accessTokenSecret = Your OAuth consumer key access token secret

- Defining Sink
  The sink for such an import is HDFS and the configuration parameters need to be accordingly set.
  TwitterAgent.sinks.HDFS.type = hdfs
  TwitterAgent.sinks.HDFS.hdfs.path = hdfs://localhost:9000/user/Hadoop/twitter_data/
  TwitterAgent.sinks.HDFS.hdfs.fileType = DataStream
  TwitterAgent.sinks.HDFS.hdfs.writeFormat = Text
  TwitterAgent.sinks.HDFS.hdfs.batchSize = 1000
  TwitterAgent.sinks.HDFS.hdfs.rollSize = 0
  TwitterAgent.sinks.HDFS.hdfs.rollCount = 10000
- Defining Channel
  The channel in this case will be the memory channel.
  TwitterAgent.channels.MemChannel.capacity = 10000
  TwitterAgent.channels.MemChannel.transactionCapacity = 100
- Binding Source and Sink to Channel
  TwitterAgent.sources.Twitter.channels = MemChannel
  TwitterAgent.sinks.HDFS.channel = MemChannel

The following command must be given to start the Flume agent –

$bin/flume-ng agent --conf ./conf/ -f conf/twitter.conf
Dflume.root.logger=DEBUG,console -n TwitterAgent

Here,

agent – Command to start the Flume agent
--conf,-c<conf> – Use configuration file in the conf directory
-f<file> – Specifies a config file path, if missing
--name, -n <name> – Name of the twitter agent
-D property =value – Sets a Java system property value.

If everything goes as expected, streaming of data should begin. To check the imported data, you can visit the link –

http://localhost:50070/

Go to the Utilities tab on the top panel menu and browse the file system.

Chapter 20

PROJECT

Now that you are thorough with the basics of Big Data and Hadoop, you are ready to take up a use case and apply the learning to implement a viable solution. To start with, a Hadoop project will require you to answer three questions –

- How will you import data?
- Which programming environment is best suited for implementing a solution for a problem at hand (MapReduce/Pig/Hive)?
- What is the expected output and how will you present the same to the user?

A sample problem definition is – finding top 10 rated links per category. The input in this case will be XML files with data line reviews. A project like this shall require the use of different tools and techniques for different function implementations. For example, the following flow may be used –

- The unstructured data can be imported into HDFS using Flume. However, if it is available in the form of a file, a command-line import may also be done.
- In view of the fact that this data is completely unstructured and it may not be suitable for tools like Pig and Hive to process this data, MapReduce programming can be used to add structure to

this data. This shall include XML parsing to divide raw data into structured data.

- Henceforth, Pig can be used for performing categorization of how links are being rated by people.
- The top ten rating for a category can be simply determined using a SQL-like Hive query on top of Pig.
- The structured information can be dumped back to MySQL for reporting using Sqoop.

In other words, for any project, you have to first define the workflow and then identify tools and techniques that will befit the required functionality. To help you make this choice, let us give you a summary of where MapReduce/Hive/Pig can be used and where their use should be avoided.

	When To Use	**When To Avoid**
MapReduce	• Data is extremely unstructured (XML files) • The problem statement requires complex logic implementation. • MapReduce can be used for both structured as well as unstructured data.	• Cannot be used for joining tables. Therefore, if a solution requires join implementation, MapReduce must be avoided. • It is complex and requires time. Therefore, if a problem requires quick solution, MapReduce may not be the best option to go for.
Pig	• Pig is considered best for semi-structured data processing. However, it can be used for both structured and unstructured data.	• The use of Pig must be avoided when you are working with smaller datasets, as the overheads involved will compromise the performance of the solution.

	When To Use	When To Avoid
Hive	• Hive should be used for applications like adhoc analysis. • Hive is recommended for developers who have experience of working in SQL. • Hive implementation requires minimum time and is a good solution for applications that require a quick solution.	• Hive is an appropriate solution only for structured data. Therefore, it should not be used for other types of data. • Hive is not recommended for complex problems.

Some project ideas have been given below. However, you can feel free to explore the different applications of Hadoop in any walk of life where you feel a solution can be beneficial to the people involved.

- Health Sector
  One of the most popular use cases for Big Data and Hadoop implementation is the health sector. You can take the patient feedback data for different hospitals to determine the ratings of hospitals. Moreover, you can also view top 10 hospitals or hospitals that got have a feedback score equal or more than 75%.
- Travel Industry
  Data can be analyzed to determine the top travel destinations for a season. Moreover, an analysis of which destinations generate maximum revenue in which season can also be made.
- Customer Support
  The dataset for customer support can be used to get a cumulative analysis of the number of complaints that are filed on a daily basis; the number of complaints that are processed and the feedback received for the processed complaints.

- Education Analytics
  The teacher information for institutions can be used to determine a region-wise analysis of the number of male and female teachers in primary and higher education institutions.

The provided examples are just tip of the iceberg when it comes to the wide range of applications that are possible in these domains. Moreover, you can explore other domains also to develop innovative solutions in this area of research.

Appendix

MCQ – ANSWERS

Chapter 1 –
1. d
2. c
3. a

Chapter 2 –
1. b
2. a
3. d

Chapter 3 –
1. d
2. b
3. c

Chapter 4 –
1. a
2. d

Chapter 5 –
1. c
2. d
3. c
4. d

Chapter 6 –
1. b
2. b
3. c
4. c

Chapter 7 –
1. d
2. a
3. a
4. c

Chapter 8 –
1. a
2. c
3. d

Chapter 9 –
1. d
2. d

INDEX

www.ingramcontent.com/pod-product-compliance
Ingram Content Group UK Ltd.
Pitfield, Milton Keynes, MK11 3LW, UK
UKHW041855190726
13854UKWH00002B/925

9 798885 304870